T0147005

BOOTCAMP IN MIRACLES

SCIENCE AND SPIRITUALITY
MINDFUL WORKOUT FOR
UNDERSTANDING THE A
COURSE IN MIRACLES.

MONNICA GARCIA

BALBOA.
PRESS

A DIVISION OF HAY HOUSE

Scriptures were taken from KJV

Balboa Press books may be ordered through booksellers or by contacting:

Balboa Press
A Division of Hay House
1663 Liberty Drive
Bloomington, IN 47403
www.balboapress.com
1 (877) 407-4847

Because of the dynamic nature of the Internet, any web addresses or
links contained in this book may have changed since publication and
may no longer be valid. The views expressed in this work are solely those
of the author and do not necessarily reflect the views of the publisher,
and the publisher hereby disclaims any responsibility for them.

The author of this book does not dispense medical advice or prescribe the use
of any technique as a form of treatment for physical, emotional, or medical
problems without the advice of a physician, either directly or indirectly. The
intent of the author is only to offer information of a general nature to help
you in your quest for emotional and spiritual well-being. In the event you use
any of the information in this book for yourself, which is your constitutional
right, the author and the publisher assume no responsibility for your actions.

Any people depicted in stock imagery provided by Getty Images are
models, and such images are being used for illustrative purposes only.
Certain stock imagery © Getty Images.

Print information available on the last page.

ISBN: 978-1-9822-1383-1 (sc)
ISBN: 978-1-9822-1385-5 (hc)
ISBN: 978-1-9822-1384-8 (e)

Library of Congress Control Number: 2018911934

Balboa Press rev. date: 10/05/2018

Contents

Preface vii

Introduction xi

Understanding Divine Order. 1

What About ACIM? 3

The Science Behind the Journey 12

Neuroscience. 20

Consciousness 24

Psychology Shaping Perception 27

Religions, Metaphisics and Spirituality Intertwining
with Science 36

PART 2

Life Parables and its Miracles. 47

Bibliography 95

PREFACE

Life constantly guides us, teaching patiently how one can evolve. Keeping oneself spiritually conscious to attain pure awareness takes willingness and commitment, similarly to a fitness regimen. This is only an analogy as an inner 'work' is not about getting better but about remembering what we really are. Accordingly, same as a person cannot expect to attain an athletic body by solely reading fitness magazines, the words and ideas on spiritual wisdom will only serve the intellect if not put into practice. Results are proportional to the discipline implicated, and the result we are referring to here is an Awakening.

This inner work may feel like a Boot Camp struggle at times, but is only so until correcting our perception becomes a consistent practice and second nature. This we could call the ultimate healthy lifestyle! Like exercise, once we overcome our limiting conditionings and resistance, a sense of empowerment and bliss is experienced. In a self-realization journey, this is the outcome of a healed perception; which is the fundamental source of miracles.

In this material, I will share with you my personal steps towards a "spiritual boot camp". The first part of the book, I am basically pointing out how my rational mind and passion for psychology, Quantum Physics and mysticism led me to understand and select the A Course In Miracles (ACIM) as my constant spiritual discipline. The second part I am highlighting what I recall, perceive and feel relevant in the process of putting this knowledge into practice. These are every-day situations where I am brainstorming and processing what affects me, as an opportunity for healing the mind. This practical process is called forgiveness in the ACIM.

But before I start getting too methodological or too mystical, let me tell you a little bit about myself.

I was born in the US and raised in Brazil since I was four years old. Thanks to my American father, I was brought up with a tad of skepticism and inquisitiveness. Thanks to my mother, I was nurtured with an abundance of beliefs and religious diversity. I was educated among nuns in a girls-only catholic school most of my childhood. Externally, I was a model student and very well behaved, but inside I used to question a lot of what I used to hear from the 'religious authorities".

Outside the school, things were not so conventional. Brazil has a very diverse demography with many races and ethic groups. Within this scenario, I was exposed to many different beliefs ranging from African rituals to Buddha, angels and crystals.

Nevertheless, don't assume anything crazy; I essentially grew up pretty "normal", simply very curious about all religions, mysticism and self-help books. I understand most may not think these pursues as normal, so perhaps I was just a competent chameleon, capable of blending in with my peers.

Details aside, my academics took on its course. I did well in school, good in high school, and made it pretty decently through college. To get my bachelors degree, however, I put aside my passion for Physical Education and graduated from Business Administration. Nevertheless, shortly after graduation I moved to the U.S. and smoothly got involved in the fitness industry. From that point on, things started to happen and this period of my life flourished better than I could have ever expected.

To this date, I've been a successful personal trainer for over 20 years. Fortunately, my curriculum includes many big shots and celebrities among Latin and American models, actors, singers, music and movie producers. I collaborated in many online articles, interviewed celebrities for the past Shape en Espanol magazine, co-hosted an early morning television segment and appeared as guest in radio, television and public events.

On the obvious course of things, my potential was - and is - to become a famous trainer. But oddly, the more intimate I had become with my wealthy and celebrity clients, the less interested I got in becoming rich-and-famous myself. Furthermore, all the social media fitness superstars started to nauseate me instead of becoming an inspiration.

In order to find more "substance" to my career, I started to take health and nutrition more seriously. Later, I found a niche where I could target other matters dear to me. I started to integrate food for health, fitness and environmental concerns, in practical and sustainable ways. I was happy and inspired to combine these cherished principles while making it accessible to every one.

As a result, I ended up writing a simple and unique book about this meaningful nutritional concept. After a few years of resistance, dramas, time consumed, money spent, joys and pains to finish the project, something happened in the 11th hour. Instead of feeling like celebrating, I notified my publisher I no longer wanted to release that book!

After a period of self-reflection, I realized I was no longer prioritizing those topics, neither seeing myself as a "nutritional warrior". To make a long story short, I told my publisher I was going to focus on my "soul's nutrition" and start to write about what was now resonating with me. Part of me was discouraged to start from scratch, but I felt it was the right thing to do. This new writing is this book — a modest description of what led me to this journey and the process that is keeping me in it. I wish this work would inspire others and myself in persisting and 'working out' on the mindset of Self-realization.

"In youth we learn, in age we understand"
Marie von Ebner-Eschenbach

INTRODUCTION

I actually started the ACIM (which I will simply call the 'Course') after reading the book The Disappearance of the Universe (DU) by Gary Renard. Interestingly, when my best friend Lou gifted it to me, something looked familiar. As I got home, I noticed I already had the book sitting on my shelf, unread. It is very common to hear about people being introduced to the Course through this book. The great about the DU is that one can immediately understand and practice the Course's fundamentals even before reading the extensive ACIM contents. Concurrently, I started to go through the lessons of the Course (which took me over two years to complete) and since then Lou and I would debate and analyze many of our life's issues together. With time we became each other's best therapist and mighty companions.

While going through the Course lessons, I would unmethodically go over its textbook and stay involved in Hindu teachings and techniques that always fascinated me, along anything to do with Yogananda. After a couple of years on this shared interests, I was listening to a Hindu guru Ted-Talk when I came across another interesting YouTube video. It was this chubby, happy, talkative guy and a sweet Asian lady sitting by a fireplace. Their presence and commentaries captivated me, and I started searching for more and more videos from this delightful ACIM teacher. I am referring to David Hoffmeister, an amazing modern-day mystic who lives the Course principles in a lovely, joyful and uncompromising way.

What happened next was guidance towards embracing the Course, which I only came to understand some time later. Listening to David made me question 'if's and 'how's to adapt other disciplines to the Course principals. As a quick response from the "Divine Universe" I met a guy from India who was extremely devoted to Hindu philosophies, rituals, scriptures, breathing techniques, chanting, mudras and meditation. We immediately felt this was a match made in heaven. I later realized it was a match made for my discernment.

As I was listening to David and his comprehensive, loving and uncompromising clarifications of the Course, I started to understand non-dualism, the mind, Maya and how to incorporate these contexts to day-to-day life. In contrast, I was witnessing my Hindu match immersed on deeply rooted emotional problems, psychosomatic physical conditions, judgments, rules, attachments and a fanatic ritualistic pattern that I didn't see doing much for his restless state of mind. The contrast of David's blissful ways and my companion's dutiful gloomy presence was the symbolic sign I needed to steer me to one direction. I realized it was time to follow one of the two paths to progress. I felt I could only master surfing a great wave standing solely on one surfing board! The situations I found myself observing were the perfect environment to know which one it was. Ironically, our paths and life circumstances split apart. He went back to India and I dived profoundly into the ACIM. This was November of 2016.

The following month, my spiritual dedication went up another notch. I made listening to David Hoffmeister a daily commitment to get inspired and understand how to apply the knowledge and non-dualistic fundamentals of the Course into everyday life situations. In this tone, I started the year of 2017 with a great resolution – a strong determination to focus on my self-realization. This term is also referred to as awakening ("waking up") and enlightenment (finding the light within).

As a New Year resolution commitment, I purchased an ACIM retreat in Utah in the first few days of January. Because of my disciplined fitness career, I felt that a few days of isolation would give me more focus and perseverance on my new 'task', just like a weight loss spa getaway would boost, adjust and motivate someone into a healthier routine. I felt doing it 'my way' and keeping a balance between the two worlds (worldly routines and spirituality) could only take me so far.

Because of my professional background, I often use metaphors between fitness and spirituality to make a point or simplify understanding. Getting fit is a process, as well as becoming more conscious or aware in order to 'awake'. But how 'triumphant' the process will be depends on one's willingness and discipline.

Within this theme, I reflect on a metaphor. Lets take Michael

Phelps as an example. We all know he became one of the greatest swimmers in the world. Do you think he had a balanced life? Do you think he was balancing his life between a job to pay his bills, time to watch television, play video games, and hang out at the bar with buddies? No! That young man was thinking and dedicating his life to swimming 24/7: inside or outside the pool. From how much food to eat, what commitments to take, how many hours to train, what gears to purchase - everything about his life was about swimming! Was his success a result of a balanced life? One can choose to be just a swimmer or the best in the world. Equally, one can choose to be a 'spiritual junkie' or Self-realized.

Can we name a great spiritual leader without a fervent, dedicated life? When you are serious about what you want to do or be in life, there's no set of scales, there's only a constant pursue for what you want. As I was sharing these thoughts, I was rephrasing those facts to myself. I remind 'Monica' how we "busy human beings" hardly set aside 10% of our lifetime for non-material, soul-meaningful aspirations. Most of it perhaps happens when we fall sick or feel unhappy. But I was promising myself not to set for so little - raise the bar, the barbells and the bells for Heaven!

I also noticed another different aspect within, which had a lot to do with getting more clarity about the Course and non-duality through David's dedicated life and discussions. My past search in spirituality was basically towards personal improvements: having more prosperity, success, health, beauty, happiness and romance. Moreover, I was striving to make people improve themselves (fitness and nutrition) and make Earth a better place (animal and environment care, politics). But with the current understanding, my goal and purpose has changed from focusing on a "better illusion" to getting out of the illusion.

This is why renouncing to my nutritional book was fundamental. It would force me to converge my focus away from what I was comfortable and convinced with (professional routines, health-related 'facts') to think and act from awareness (see beyond the deceptive conditioning). It would be a renouncement to a dear identity (persona) and beliefs that shaped my life for so many years. It was like a forced rehabilitation program for the ego.

Soul-time is so limited nowadays. The time spent in harmony with our true (divine) essence becomes so limited that no wonder people are more and more feeling unfulfilled, unhappy, depressed, anxious and so on. The spirit revives, and the ego destroys. Why would I 'perk up' my career for a busy demand of wellness workshops, promotions, social media and events with affairs that have nothing to do with my real purpose in life? It would only be a set of 'new and improved' set of rules and routines that imprison. Morpheus makes the perfect statement when telling Neo "You are a prisoner of your mind", in the movie The Matrix. We need constant reminders and discipline to set oneself free, not more distractions and disillusions.

Please understand I am just beginning this journey! I am not here to preach anything or tell you how to "know thy self". I am only getting started and may have a long way to go (hopefully I am mistaken). Nevertheless, my intention is to share the themes and episodes of my life that had me discern the Course from other paths, understand the lessons and process the healing opportunities life throws at me.

UNDERSTANDING DIVINE ORDER

So after renouncing the book, I went through a phase of uncertainty, anxiety and gloominess, which are all branches of fear. For a good reason our old ways are called comfort-zones. I was hopeful that my February retreat in Utah would clarify things for me. Paradoxically, I missed the flight. Looking back with right-minded vision, this 'misfortune' was an expression, in form, of all the distressful thoughts and feelings I was having previous to my trip. After a few days of feeling horrible, correcting my thoughts, blaming and forgiving myself, I finally started to experience all things working together for good.

Our ignorance of the higher purpose or the 'better way' is what gives us pain. Is like a child throwing a tantrum because the parent is not letting him touch the electrical outlet to play. If the child had the understanding that the "punishing restriction" was for his best, he would immediately be thankful for it. This is comparable to all the stuff we get upset about. However, if we keep exercising the mind to accept that drama is unnecessary and wait gracefully for the best outcomes, all start to change for the best.

Months later, I saw the bigger picture. First of all, I was being too hard on myself. It was like planning to be in the next National tennis tournament when only starting to learn the sport. I was not ready to drastically change my life. Like getting ready for a championship, the process comes gradually until one feels so confident playing the sport that becoming a pro comes naturally. Likewise, one needs to feel self-assured, or fully guided, before deciding to take any big spiritual leap.

Slowly I began to ask for guidance to put things into perspective. Gradually, concerns turned to clarity. Like my upset about the time and money invested to write my nutritional book was replaced with a new understanding. It was all to practice and feel confident to write this book. Plus, the publishing contract and investments were crucial to force myself to commit and publicize this personal journey. Little by little, more clarity, ideas, lessons and directions started to take shape towards my new *course* of life.

Missing that flight was decisive in setting the ground for gradual changes. Didn't all my childhood and life events gradually lead me to this point? Didn't all I came across regarding science, spiritual wisdom and psychology lead me to this perspective and awareness of life? All things indeed work together for good. Everything *is* in Divine Order.

WHAT ABOUT ACIM?

Plenty material is available in books and videos about what is the A Course In Miracles (ACIM) and how it came about. This is a short overview highlighting the key points of how, why and what has been meaningful for my fondness and choice of the Course as my primary spiritual direction.

For me, the ACIM is a complete package to heal the mind, restore the soul and know thyself, as it intertwines cherished elements like psychology, spiritual wisdom, and science fundamentals. The Course is a primordial wisdom with Christian and psychological terms. This path is not about faith but awareness and understanding of the complex human condition controlled by the mind and its ego thought system. The Course is utterly practical and its practice is not apart from our perceived daily reality. The Course is not something we do on spare times or Sunday mornings. This is an everyday, 24/7 commitment to see life differently. It is not about what we do or preach, but about what we think and feel. It is not about how we act in the world, but about how and what we think, perceive and extend to it. The Course aims and guides us from within. It essentially and diligently focuses on the mind and on disciplining it so we can remember and recognize what we are. We were created in the image and likeness of God, which means we are pure spirit. The Course discloses how all our limitations and distortions are in the mind due to erroneous human programming. Therefore, corrections are targeted within our psyche; not on rules, rituals and obligations. This goes along with the teachings of Ho'oponopono, which is all about 'cleaning' the 'data' in the mind to allow Divinity to express through us. I embrace its simplicity and apply it often.

The surreal and intellectual prose of the Course is not an easy read for many, which makes having a notion in non-dualistic philosophies, psychology and Quantum Physics the perfect tools to pre-digest and encourage a true commitment to the process. These intertwining elements were exactly what awestruck me so profoundly. But this is because of my brainy personality. Actually, to understand non-duality, knowing how to count till one is beyond necessary!

The ACIM is not a religion, although is feasibly an equivalent to the Vedanta (ancient Hindu philosophy) with Christian terminology in a timeless Shakespearian speech. The Course can be seen as an approach that integrates mystical and practical aspects of human experiences with the context of modern psychology. For a brief description, it can be called a transformational "spiritual psychotherapy" - the optimum wake up call!

So how did this masterwork material come about? It all

started back in 1965 with two clinical and research psychologists at Colombia University Medical center, Helen Schucman and her boss William Thetford. These two professors became the original scribers of the ACIM after a series of interesting experiences and until a persistent voice was speaking through Helen's mind. I found interesting the fact she was not welcoming what was going on (as a psychologist, one that hears voices in the head has a degree of psychosis), and that she was a Jewish-raised atheist well known for her difficult personality. These qualities are completely diverse from the gentle, compassionate and loving nature of the Course. Furthermore, the scribe took long seven years to be completed as Helen's attempts to intervene with personal impressions were constantly being rectified by the 'dictating voice', which she soon recognized as Jesus. Additionally amazing and out-of-this-world was to find out the majority of the 'tutorial' material of the Course (lesson 98 to 365th) is written in traditional Iambic Pentameter, as if this complex style was arranged to feel like poetry to the soul.

The ACIM material is practically a reinstatement of ancient wisdom based on non-duality, which tells us that the world, time and space we live in is not the ultimate reality. Moreover, it is not where happiness dwells until we start to change and 'reprogram' our minds. In a figurative manner, the Course could be looked at it as a spiritual psychological method to rectify and rewire all the garbage and mistaken beliefs we were set to make out about the world and ourselves. No need to worry about this being a brainwashing course, but gladly be aware it certainly is a mind-washing curriculum. Correcting all the inaccurate information we have involuntary established to rule our lives with, we start to allow all guilt and pain to vanish from our experience. The Course requires a profound spiritual awareness and discipline, but unlike a religion, it is vastly described as a self-study course. From a psychological standpoint, it is a practice that allows rewiring our minds from a fear-driven life to a love-driven one. From a scientific standpoint, it takes us from a Newtonian cause-and-effect perspective of life to a Quantum effect-and-cause stance.

Personally, I asked myself why didn't Jesus speak with this depth before? Primary, the Course's message could only be introduced and understood by humanity, in totality, after Sigmund Freud's tripartite model of the mind and its ego functioning elements. Carl Jung further enriched this archetypal with concepts of collective consciousness and unconsciousness, which are now being implemented to unwind our minds back to Oneness, or the Mind of God. But even so, Jesus did address projection and denial when he said to not look at the speck of a brother's eye when one has a plank in our own eye.

Furthermore, today we can better understand how Quantum Mechanics are involved in each individual's perception of reality. Correspondingly, the ACIM clarifies how everything is a concept in the mind; how all we see is a projection of our inner state and how all the feelings we experience (anger, fear, excitement, sadness) are emotional reactions coming from a false self-identification. Accordingly, how far could his message go if Jesus was talking about a psychological holographic nature of reality when no one could even imagine the planet being round?

True vision is to see the Oneness in everyone rather than believing what the senses show us. The conceptual mind of reality (materialism) is but an assumption and the only reason stopping us from seeing and experiencing our true nature as One with God (Christ Mind, Buddha within, Sonship). I'll take this opportunity to disclose a couple of major concepts I had to re-evaluate from my catholic upbringing and cultural convention. First, God is not a person-like creature setting rules and right-from-wrongs. God is Infinite Creation (Quantum Field), pure abstraction of light and love. Second, we are not billions of souls inside bodies. This concept gives us the erroneous sense of individuality. We are one spirit created in the image and likeness of God (Sonship) perceiving multiplicity (dreaming) because of the ego though system of separation. We are one in God (non-dualism). Third, Christ is not synonym for Jesus. Christ is a word for God's creation, the Sonship in His quantum mind. Because Jesus recognized his true spiritual identity, his name became associated with the Christ Mind and 'the' Son of God. Forth, the world we live in is not reality. Reality is what God creates. Because (S)He creates as Himself, true reality is only of infinite-spiritual nature. Equally, the ego creates as itself. Created and contained by a thought system, this world is nothing but a dream-like illusion. Within our perception, the Creator extends and the ego projects. This corresponds to Ho'oponopono that says we live either from data memory (ego) or from inspiration (divine insight). These concepts are important to remind myself of, as it is relevant for understanding the fundamental meaning of some words used in the Course.

As a personal trainer with spiritual values, I was always seeking for a body/mind/spirit balance. The Course, interestingly, focuses exclusively on the mind where the Holy Spirit (Higher Self or Consciousness) abides as a bridge to our unified Divine Consciousness (Christ Mind). But this is not a bridge to link and balance the body and spirit, but to appoint and split them completely apart once we decide to cross it! This was intricate for me at first as even Buddhism and Hinduism, where I had looked for answers before, show some levels of confusion portraying dualistic human interpretations on non-dualistic fundamentals. This includes the efforts to make this world a better place or to enhance our life here on Earth. Like the alluring Law of Attraction, it becomes a Law of Attachment (or Distraction) that keeps us bond and mesmerized with the outside world; it offers nothing for spiritual progress. I can say this distraction law works very well as I engaged it for many years; it is all about goals, control and power. The course is about purpose, guidance and trust.

After much effort to understand and acquire the sought for body/mind/soul balance, the Course eradicates this flawed notion making sure we understand the body and the soul are mutually excludable. There are, however, many Course teachers that still try to incorporate dualism and balance into the illusion. But always go back to what the Course discloses and, above all, ask for holy guidance, true vision and clear understanding. Most of the time, guidance would come as gradual adjustment as we start to look at things differently.

Personally, I am slowly steering away from dietary structures and lifestyle habits. As well, I became less enthusiastic about my Yoga practices. I feel much 'spiritualization of the body' and fashion statements go on in western practice. I still enjoy my gym workouts (not sure until when) but Yoga was something I was getting involved with expecting a 'return' I now understand is not the case. In terms of personal training, I hardly used to know about my client's personal life and was an intense military-style trainer bossing people about what to do, what do eat, etc. Now a day, I am a kinder trainer and sometimes take more care of their state of mind than their bodies.

Generally speaking, my lifelong healthy lifestyle has been my ankle of Achilles as past associations and deep-rooted beliefs are like quicksand. The more we identify with personal concepts or by what billions of people believe in, the deeper we get sucked into the illusion. Yet, a deeply engrained belief system does not make it true. Salvation (freedom, awareness) is the escape from all the false concepts we hold. The logging for balance can become a trap from the ego towards this letting-go to attain self-realization. The One Mind of God is all there is, everything else is a distraction, but we can surely be guided gradually out of our beliefs and personal preferences. The Course is a wonderful tool to guide and encourage us to remove the obstacles to the Divine Love's presence. All we are asked to do is be willing to see differently and see all illusions for what they are: a concept in the mind.

The fundamental process to 'see the false as false' referred as *Forgiveness* in the Course is very different from the ordinary impression that someone did us wrong and we forgive the other person, as 'better' human beings. The 'true forgiveness' – and the fundamental idea of the Course - is about remembering the holographic nature of reality as mental projections of our inner state. When we consciously acknowledge this, we start disempowering the dynamics of the ego and how the reflections of our inner state affect us. Neuroscience researches recognize all we feel and perceive is first a stimulus in the brain! Keep in mind the eyes do not see. We are not looking but making up images, inside our brains, from the programmed beliefs. As we go deeper into unified awareness, we realize that the mind tells the body what to see, what to hear, what to feel, and what to experience. Gradually becoming aware of the unreality of all situations (dream state), one starts to wake up.

The road to awakening is through this kind of forgiveness; it is about consciously releasing personal thoughts and false beliefs based on guilt and fear we use to give meaning to this world. When we forgive and see the false as false (true vision) we allow the correction (atonement). The instant we recognize this (holy instant) we experience the consequent miracles. Miracles are but a change in the mind, a change in perception. The more we withdraw all the meanings we assign to the world (forgive), the more vision we attain. Forgiving the falsehood we remove the psychological shadows of the ego system. With less shadows (judgments), more light is projected from within; as more light is projected, more miracles are experienced. A messenger (Holy Spirit/ Higher Self) knows we got trapped in a nightmare full of scary symbols, all based on an ontological subconscious guilt. The HS is a presence in the mind to remind us there is no objective world outside this guilty consciousness projecting a dreamingly psycho dramatic reality. The HS recaps we never split apart from

God and we still as (S)He created us – pure, divine and innocent. As we (as prodigal sons) deliberately will and allow its intervention, the HS acts as a bridge back to our divine source while guiding and whispering to us to wake up. This is a brief summary of what the Course and its curriculum encompass.

THE SCIENCE BEHIND THE JOURNEY

Many times I look back and tell myself I wish I knew this-and-that earlier in life. But then I understand this journey is like a puzzle that will be solved in its own time. No work done will be lost (on this or other time/ dimension) and the end result is sure (conscious return home) but willingness and efforts are essential in linear time.

Getting to know the basics of Quantum Physics was essential for my personal development and took my stage of learning the Course to another level. It still only a set of tools and symbols that our 'true nature' or 'source', 'higher self' or our Holy Spirit uses to get us through from the level we are on. The *What The Blip Do We Know* movie was an introduction and made me recognize and question about Consciousness. This led me to materials showing the holographic nature of everything, and conclusions of our illusive existence. Both concepts made me reflect more intensely about how the universe works and my role in life itself.

I had heard about life being an illusion in many ancient

religions, spiritual traditions and philosophy. But only after getting to know some Quantum Physics fundamentals, I finally started to grasp their principles.

When participating in ACIM study groups, I often notice people taking the information that everything is an illusion as a philosophical assumption or religious conviction. This is why I find so important to exploit scientific information to evolve these framed ideas. Furthermore, science and spiritual paths are the same thing – both are searching for the truth!

Truth is always out for those ready to take it, but acceptance and understanding is a process. Lets keep in mind how centuries ago we humans used to believe the Earth was flat. It took around 300 years for the average people (non-scholars) to accept the new reality. From the early Greek philosophers to the first astronauts on the moon, there was a long transition and slow process of understanding how Earth is really like.

We are in a middle of a cutting edge paradox. Einstein's' Relativity principle radically changed the Newtonian view of reality. Only in the past 30 years some of its concepts are being vastly accepted in the field of science and make movies like Matrix make more sense to us than ever. Taking this to our limited reality still a work in progress. However, to what concerns a spiritual journey, renowned physicists agree that the holographic conclusion is the most radical thing that has happened to our understanding of space, time and matter since the quantum mechanics came to exist.

The main light Quantum Mechanics findings brought to my understanding and "faith-based" idea about the world being

Maya (illusion) starts with the Double Slit experiment. In this quantum realm one clearly take the conclusion that reality is not how we currently understand it, but how we perceive it.

Why was this conducted experiment so revealing to my spiritual search? Because it demonstrates "existence" using subatomic particles, and that's what our "reality" is made of. We are all made of atoms. Thus, the concept applies to our existence as individuals.

To fully understand the depth and meaning of this experimentation, I did a basic science cheat sheet with the concepts that align with our task to understand our illusionary reality, consciousness and who we truly are.

Matter = Objects that take up space and have mass.
All Matter is composed of atoms.

Atoms = Foundation of all things in the universe.
Made of electrons, neutrons and protons.

Cell = Basic unit of life, "building blocks" of all living organisms.

Electron = Subatomic particle, tinny piece of matter and energy.

Waves = Disturbance that travels through space and matter transporting energy from one place to another.
They transfer energy, not matter.

Other concepts to keep in mind to comprehend the magnitude of the quantum experiment:

- Light and Energy travel in waves, as for sound waves, seismic waves and light waves within the electromagnetic spectrum.
- A cell is made of molecules and a molecule is made of Atoms.
- The human body is composed of trillions of cells. Likewise, a standard needle can be composed of billions of atoms among iron, nickel, copper and others.

Quantum Physics (QP) demonstrates some bizarre outcomes at an atomic scale. All thanks to the famous conduct experiment I mentioned earlier, the Double-Slit Experiment. The behavior of the atomic particles and the result was so perplexing that it was nicknamed "spooky action" or *mystery*, in a popular term. [1]

I encourage you to search on YouTube for visual details but here follows my description of how "spooky" and "mysterious" the results are.

When we shoot matter - like numerous pebbles - at a barrier with two slits, we get two similar slit-shaped strips on the screen where it was hit. When a wave of water goes through the same barrier with two slits, a small wave comes out of each slit becoming two waves on the other side. As each small wave expands, they interfere with each other. By the time they hit the screen, an image of many vertical strips are seen. The center one is where

---

[1] https://en.wikipedia.org/wiki/Double-slit_experiment

they hit with more intensity (visually darker) and the other ones fade as they expand to the sides. This is the visual effect of waves collapsing onto the screen trough two slits.

Next experiment was performed with electrons, so keep your cheat sheet in hand.

When shooting electrons – which science has always defined as a particle (little piece of matter) - through a barrier with two slits, we all evidently expect to see a pattern on the screen equally in shape to the two slits. But we don't! When those electrons are shot one by one through the slits, they form the same interference pattern that waves do. Mind blowing!

The shocking conclusion is that the building blocks of "reality" (the electrons in this case) behave like they are not solid at all. So, to understand the logic of this uninspected result, the same experiment was performed with a recording camera.

With its result, physicist forever entered into the bizarre world of Quantum Physics. The pattern on the screen formed a shadow-like shape of the two slits, just like it was expected at the first experiment! What?

The conclusion taken was that the act of observing caused the wave function to collapse and create the existence of matter "as anticipated" by our common sense.

In other words, electrons, which are the building blocks of what we call "reality", can exist as waves (non-solid particles) or as matter (solid particles)! What determines one way or the other is having an observer or not. This QP experiment conclusion simply unsettled the theory of everything!

Here is when the Realism concept that a physical reality

exist independent of observation was taken aback by quantum mechanics to a Idealism concept where reality is a mental construct and does not exist independent of a observation. Here is where consciousness and physical reality interconnects.

So what conclusions can we take about the material world and "us" as an observer?

Basically, our life experiences starts to resemble watching a virtual reality video. The images in the video pop in and out as we look at it. Similarly, only what we observe becomes "real", the rest are "possibilities". The fact that the observer collapses the wave functions (converts into matter) simply by observing is indicating that the observer shapes reality and the way we think and perceive can be determining what we see, smell and feel in front of us.

Considering an atom is 99.99% empty space and what we perceive as matter is not solid as believe, then what makes reality feels so "real" to us? From this question emerged the paradigm of the "Field" and the Holographic Universe.

The Field is a pure abstract potential of existence. To make a parallel, we have unnoticed electromagnetic waves all around us that, when modulated, can be perceived and heard as music. Similarly, the Field is a wave of infinite possibilities where electrons collapse as a particle (becomes "real") when it is observed.

Physicists have found that the foundation of the universe is an intelligent, non-material, vibrating universal field - like a quantum ocean of potential reality! The more physics try to grasp and explain the material world, the more the universe slips through its fingers as something increasingly abstract. This abstract field of potentialities is a dynamic intelligence and conclusions points out we are really living in a thought, conceptual universe!

"Men are only a vapor; exalted men, an illusion.

On a balance scale, they go up; together they

[weigh] less than a vapor"

Psalm 62:9

Science, however, has no conclusions or answers to the questions of where did it come from, who made it or how does it exist?

So next likely quest is to understand how our "reality" is perceived and created from the Field and all those "empty atoms"?

Most quantum physicists agree that it can be equivalent to the creation of a hologram. You can check out videos explaining how holograms are made and go into more depth by reading The Holographic Universe by Michael Talbot.

Modern technology amazed many a few years ago at a Snoop Dogg concert when Tupac appeared on stage as a hologram. Because we know that passing our hands through the image feels like air, some disbelief may arise about the holographic model of reality. However, the point that Talbot makes regarding our reality is not that we are looking at a hologram; his point is we are part of it!

Thus, many quantum physicists are concluding that what we observe, feel and call reality is essentially a holographic motion picture experienced by us *inside* of it. This explains why everything feels so realistic.

"Reality is an illusion, albeit a very

persistent one"

A. Einstein

So let me empathize that physicist are faced with this surreal model or the so-called Measurement Problem, which is the puzzling fact that an atom only becomes "something" once a conscious observer is present. Preconceived ideas of reality lead us all to assumptions and QP is challenging us to question them by showing all the flaws our structure of belief has. Physicists are opening the way for other ideas, beside Newtonian Materialism, to be considered.

Now is the moment Morpheus is telling you: "You felt your entire life that there is something wrong with the world. You don't know what it is… Do you want to know what it is? …The Matrix is the world that has been put into your eyes to blind you from the truth… You take the blue pill, the story ends. You wake up in your bed and believe whatever you want to believe. You take the red pill, you stay in Wonderland, and I show you how deep the rabbit hole goes"

NEUROSCIENCE

An observer is the key element for reality to exist, but experiencing reality occurs with our sensory receptors for vision, taste, smell, hearing and touch, which merely are electrical signals inside the brain.

Lets take vision for example, as it provides the most extensive information about the external world. We have this idea that the process of seeing is when a mass of light travels from an object to the eye, then pass through the eye lens where they are refracted and focused on the retina at the back of the eye. Here the light rays are turned into electrical signals and transmitted by neurons to the center of vision at the back of the brain. But now we know the opposite is true! The act of seeing actually takes place in the center of the brain (visual cortex) where electrical signals are decoded into images we are familiar with, like a house, a flower, or a cat. The 'outside world' can indeed be very deceiving.

The honored neurosurgeon and neurophysiologist Dr Karl Pribram found answers about brain functions, with the help of physicist Bohn. He came to infer the brain operates much like a hologram that converts wave frequencies from the quantum field into information recognizable by our senses.

We are unaware of a great deal of brain activities that maintain our body and create our awareness; yet, brain experiments are never short of incredible and fascinating results.

All we see, smell, taste, feel and hear are only experienced at its corresponded areas in the brain. Fascinating fact is that if we only imagine a sensation (like looking at a cat) it incites the same areas in the brain as if we were actually doing it. So is reality what we see with our eyes or what we experience with our brains?

Neurosurgeon Dr Benjamin Libet performed a series of experiments that became very famous. While patients were conscious and with brain exposed, he would touch their little finger, ask and observe when the stimulus was received in the cortex. Correspondingly, Dr Libet would stimulate that same area and ask the patient when was the touch felt in the finger.

The expected result was that once the finger was touched, the stimulus would travel all the way up to the brain, so the patient would report it a fraction of a second later; and when the brain was directly stimulated, the patient would feel it immediately.

But just the opposite happened! When the doctor touched the finger, the patient felt it immediately; and when the cortex got directly stimulated, the patient felt it with a delay!

Dr Libet and many scientists were astounded with these outcomes and unsatisfied with a "time reversal theory" at the time.

In another research, he wanted to measure when do we have

the conscious decision to move. Which comes first, the decision to move or the start of the brain activity?

To his amazement, he verified that the decision to move comes about 1/5 of a second before the action, and the start of the brain activity comes half a second before – more than twice as long before the action. So the brain signals 'activity' way before we make the conscious decision to move!

A further astonishing experiment was conducted wiring up collaborators with skin conductors, heart rate monitors and other devices to monitor the person's reactions. They were put in front of a screen and informed they were about to see different types of pictures, randomly selected: relaxing, happy, sad, violent, etc. The body's physiology change when the brain discerns the emotions that are provoked, so the monitors can classify when the subject is looking at something exciting, soothing, violent, and so on. The amazing result after monitoring hundreds of volunteers' shows that people were getting sad, aroused, happy, scared or excited accordingly to the images, fractions of a second before the images were appearing in front of them.

What? So this means the brain can anticipate not only what a person will observe and be aware of, but also which type of image will pop from the computer!

On a similar experiment the complexity of 'conscious decision' was added to the assessment. Inside a computerized axial tomography scanner, a person is given two control devises (right and left) to randomly press, as desired. At all time, the scanner is recording when the brain is making the decision. The result was that his conscious decision of pressing the right or left control was predicted and shown in the computer screen six seconds before he pressed the button! This was rationalized as if there is a form of deterministic mechanism unfolding that leads to a decision later in time.

This can subtlety feel frightening as our 'authority' appears secondary and one may stop to ask who is making judgments, decisions and determining our life?

What science is basically reveling is that our brains appear to know what's going to happen even before we do. Going back to QP, lets recall how an observer decodes and collapse waves from the Field into particles of 'reality' and then sends this decoded 'reality' information out to be perceived and experienced. The brain establishes what will be determined in the personal hologram (from conscious decisions to computer's random images), while the body perceives (becomes aware of) the 'out there' with a delay. As bizarre and amazing all this may sound, research after researches have nothing but confirmed these interpretations.

Lets recall how we started this neuroscience discussion and how our five senses (seeing, touching, hearing, tasting, smelling) was typically considered incoming information from the world. Now this notion is plunged with the recognition that projection (senses' signals in the brain) comes before perception (personal recognition), where the quantum waves takes shape and allow the whole holographic universe to express itself and emerge around us. This will interconnect with topics coming next and bring more clarity to some peculiar core principles of the Course.

CONSCIOUSNESS

One can be alive but not conscious. Consciousness, generally speaking, is having full activities of the mind and senses. Like being aware of one's identity or of being awake instead of sleeping. In science, consciousness gets to study the awareness of our individuality and the certainty of knowing.

The brain experiments previously addressed touched fundamentalist arguments and left scientists with more questions than answers. Nevertheless, the most intriguing aspect of all was to question free will and the power of decision-making. This subsequently led us to question who or what is determining our life by shaping specific wave frequencies as the "real world" we experience?

The best answer scientists have agreed on is 'consciousness', sustaining it is what is choosing specific frequencies from the quantum field. Only conscious beings can be observers, therefore we are intimately tied to the very existence of reality.

Without conscious beings, all would just be a quantum soup - an expanding superposition of possibilities with nothing definitive ever happening.

Because of its unempirical nature and somehow worrying about their professional reputation, some scientists get discreet exploring the subject. Nevertheless, they all see that consciousness is what is affecting the reality we live in, which is not as tangible as what appears or is believed to be.

Consciousness is so complex and so interconnected with philosophical means that it gets very challenging for scientists to define or explain it. Here is where terminology may encounter a great gap between technical and idealistic approaches. Yet, many physicists are accepting this intangible field as a spiritual realm downloading information to the human brain, where the mind consciousness converts the quanta particles into "reality".

"The more I study science, the more I believe
in God"
A. Einstein

I agree with Eckhart Tolle and many other non-dualistic teachers about not using the words Christ or God to refer to the ultimate Consciousness, Pure Awareness or the Infinite Creator. This is because these words have centuries of programming, references and associations that may be difficult to unwind the mind from. However, I occasionally use them as the Course refers to these concepts from a Christian standpoint.

I am not getting technical myself, as the purpose of all this information I am sharing with you is for the purpose of showing how QP helped me to understand some fundamental principals of the ACIM like the world being an illusion, the means of projections, the script, and so on. Nevertheless, from this point on, one has to choose which direction and language most identifies with - as for metaphysics, religion or spirituality - to understand this Consciousness responsible for collapsing our personal reality.

PSYCHOLOGY SHAPING PERCEPTION

I felt in love with psychology on my early twenties, when I first got connected with it. It took me one year to finally get a placement on a competitive and highly regarded private college in my hometown. On my second year of Business Administration, I started to have second thoughts. Even though I liked my college, teachers and friends very much, the only thing I was passionate about was nutrition and anything to do with exercise – from magazines to physiology. So halfway through my bachelor's program, I told my mom I wanted to pursue Physical Education instead.

As expected, my mother freaked out and after many debates, I agreed to take an aptitude test before taking any actions. Blessed, I got introduced to an amazing psychologist (I later realized she was a nun) who analyzed my test results. Soon after this, we started having weekly therapy sessions. This was one of the best things that happened to me. Not only she was helping me with clarity and confidence, but she would frequently lend me psychology books to read. Ironically and divinely, I was also being introduced to Carl Jung in college. I was fascinated and so not aware it was changing my life. Many years later, I am amazed and grateful to realize how psychology still enriches my life, objective and spiritually.

Psychology is often considered a "soft science" since measuring people's happiness, behaviors, and so on, are not defined and measurable like shapes and numbers are. Scientists generally overlook psychology referring to it as a field that does not grasp the truth. Nevertheless, psychology is a social science that uses scientific methodology to observe, record and measure behaviors to understand how we perceive events and make decisions.

We constantly assume everybody is seeing and experiencing the world as we do. But really? To keep it simple and straightforward, have you ever noticed differing book reviews, contradictory movie critics and conflicting opinions about a public figure? An individual's experience feels vast and splendid, however it is significantly constricted.

How we perceive the world is deeply associated with our psyche – the mental or psychological structure mediating our responses to the environment. And this structure is what molds our perception of the world. What the brain is constantly showcasing in front of us, observers, is not a simple and limiting sensory input but a complex mental interpretation of conditioning memories that pre-establishes a personal experience.

Our perception of the environment is filtered by personal upbringing that defines and initiates fears, guilt and limiting beliefs as a mental programming. The subconscious mind becomes a databank of learned behaviors. It is said that at least 95% of our life is controlled by the habits of the subconscious mind. This can be useful for mechanical tasks like getting out of bed or driving, but very restricting when it comes to thriving physically, mentally or spiritually.

As adults, we have high and low ranges of mental activities going on at all times. The lowest frequency (delta) is found in the first two years of life and is when we are only observing and watching the world go by without the ability to respond to it. Adults are in delta frequency when in deep sleep. From two to six years old the frequency increases (theta) and is where imagination starts taking place - reason why kids at this age mix imagination and the real world when they play. Adults are in theta when in light meditation or napping. At the age of six the frequency increases again (alpha) adding a calm state of consciousness. Adults are in alpha frequency when in deep relaxation. When a child reaches twelve, it had developed - and it can access - all four ranges of frequencies: delta, theta, alpha and beta. Beta is the frequency of reasoning and wakens consciousness.

The first six years are the "programmable" states when we are practically being hypnotized. This is the period of enculturation - downloading and learning the "facts you need to know" to fit in the family, society, and so on. Until this point we are like learning sponges easily absorbing and retaining all information into the subconscious. But when a circus elephant is tighten to a pole since baby and grows to be limited to move by that pole, is it being taught or programmed to act like that? When you tell a child he is playing with a broom and not a horse, are you teaching or programming the child with that data? Aren't we programmed to see, behave and judge all we experience as other people dictated us to? If you have an idea of the wonders and severity of Artificial Intelligence (AI), you are surely getting the point by now. A nice movie to see this content without swirling into an apocalyptical story is Robot and Frank – sweet and profound.

After this programming phase and beta frequency immersion, our actions become totally habitual, practically only playing back what we 'learned'. How ironic that we say "so-and-so presses my buttons" when they activate something uncomfortable for us to deal with! Troubles arise when someone is pressing "play" to a program that does not match our primitive encoding. The only way to stop the recorded conditioning from affecting us is to realize (be conscious) of what it is: a past association that is threatening our persona - our ego.

Ego psychology is perhaps the most important and enduring of Freud's contribution to modern psychology, which became more deeply defined and refined by Carl Jung. Although differing, their theories are the roots of how we analyze and understand the human mind. The outstanding fact about Jung is that he paid significant attention to Eastern philosophy and mysticism that reflected on his notion of 'self' and collective unconsciousness for his personality theories. He had also spoken about an "imprinted" characteristic that a person would be born with as a "virtual image" of oneself. Thanks to Freud and Jung, modern psychology can recognize and study the thoughts, memories and emotions that give the ego identity and continuity (personality self).

The physical world we perceive is a continuous reflection of the past, which is just a memory - an ever-changing remembrance based on a trichotomy (three elements) system as body, mind and soul. Interestingly, the Course, as a spiritual/mind training program, mentions we are always reliving the past. It makes clear its intention is to get us out of this spinning wheel and take our mind back to our God source. When looking at the world, we perceive it physically (material experience), emotionally (who we believe and feel we are) and mentally (with our thoughts, ideas and dreams). They shape our behaviors (how we interact with reality) and our beliefs (how we define our reality).

> "We are what we think. All we are arises with our thoughts, with our thoughts we make the world"
> Gautama Buddha

The subconscious mind leads us to perceive and experience reality out of our encoding, which is usually very limiting. I never forget a picture on the Internet of a horse being held by a rope looped to a cheap plastic chair that the animal could easily drag away. This is what conditioning beliefs do to us. We are as great as how we believe we are!

In evolution, a small and frontal piece of the brain (cortex) gives rise to consciousness. Consciousness is not activated mindlessly, but once accessed, it can be very creative and transformative. Whatever we don't consciously control or 'will for', the subconscious mind does! So we can choose to stay tied to conditioning beliefs (like the horse to the chair) and go on with 95% of four lives on subconscious automatic pilot, or we can exercise "awareness" and consciously experience our full potential and inherited Consciousness (purposely in capital letter).

In psychology and among mystical and spiritual leaders, self-consciousness or personal identity is recognized as the ego. Traditional spiritual paths have always referenced to practicing awareness to raise consciousness about our divinity and the knowing of our true identity or Self – which is the infinite Consciousness, the Oneness, or the Mind of God. Becoming aware of our divine nature and rising above the ego (persona concepts) is what mystics call enlightenment, Self-realization or awakening.

When gurus, monks or Saints from any religious paths are said to give up "carnal things in the world", they are not denying their humanity, but giving up their psychological defenses, deceptions and attachments to the universal illusion. The personal identity, material possessions and pursues are defense distractions used to suppress and hide the weaknesses and vulnerability of the ego, rather than turning to the infinite Oneness for support and awakening.

The Course is almost like a mind technology revealing how the ego dynamics collapses Quanta. In other words, it makes us understand how all this personality programming described so far shapes our illusory world and what we experience from it. The Course guides us to recognize the false as false and to not be deceived by the ego's virtual reality plot. But if the message is simple why does the book is so big and feels so complicated? This is because we are complex schizophrenics (withdrawn from our true reality) and the 'treatment' is proportionally complex. Plus, the ego is fighting for its life. The mind is so invested and addicted to the ego that it takes a lot of work and willingness to expose it. Our egotistic perception needs to be exposed and mistranslated to heal.

I was fascinated to observe how this plays out so true when watching a television show on the life of princess Diana. Before all this profound understanding, I used to ask how come a person so special and adored around the world could be so miserable, insecure and cornered into an unloving marriage. So I learned Diana's parents split up when she was only six years old. The divorce, custody battle and strained stepmother relationship left great emotional scars on her. Feeling ripped apart, unworthy and unloved, Diana always longed for love and a united family. With more details of her childhood one can see the roots (psychological programming) of her dramatic life plot of betrayal, loneliness, insecurity and home inconsistency. We are all projecting a motion picture and acting up some unconscious beliefs. Just like a night dream, our life scripts are all related to unconsciousness!

More recently, I got absorbed into watching a television show on celebrity autopsies as the forensic examinations to get to know the reasons of their death tell more about how they lived than why they died. They are all so similar. Hollywood prodigies and entertainment icons like Judy Garland, Elizabeth Taylor, Marilyn Monroe, James Dean, Britney Murphy, River Phoenix, Prince, Heath Ledger, Robin Williams, Philip Seymour, Whitney Houston, Elvis Presley, Amy Winehouse, Kurt Cobain,

Michael Jackson, among many others, were so in denial and disconnected from their innermost tribulations that they all ended up embracing reckless conducts and damaging lifestyles. Fame, money, power, busy schedules, self-improvements, are all fools' gold of the ego. Physical and emotional pains are a call for love. Sadly, these tragic celebrity stories I am using as 'case scenarios' constantly numbed the repercussions of their childhood scars and growing-up emotional pains with psychotropic medication, painkillers, sleeping pills and/or mind-altering drugs. Today, the "American Dream" nation holds a leadership on opioid epidemic with more than two million dependent people and a death toll that averages 115 overdoses each day. [2] Escapism, in any form, does not heal the mind as the ego programming needs to be addressed and rewired within one's consciousness.

The ego script consumes like quicksand thus, we must stay alert about devious, childish, sabotaging and victimizing thoughts, which are nothing but mechanisms to obscure the ontological guilt and fear showing up in our lives. Our beliefs, values and past wounds are imprisoning mental concepts that must be questioned and exposed to the light for healing. Uncovering and unwinding is the way out, otherwise we are nothing but terrified six year olds pretending to be sensible, responsible adults. The Course is pointing this out when it mentions we have been poorly taught. Life can be a classroom and the body a radar detector that discloses where the real suffering is - in the mind. The way out of this vicious loop, or "cure", is what the Course calls Salvation. The true healing can only come from outside the ego's thought

---

[2] Wikipedia Opioid Epidemic, en.m.wikipedia.org

system – a spiritual source or the Holy Spirit (HS) – because is the presence in our mind that overlooks the falsehood (forgive).

Because we never question if all we learned in our growing years were false or not, we end up building a false version of who we truly are. The Course's "spiritual psychology" and knowledge can change this as it targets and dissipates all our psychological garbage. Our defenses and misperceptions must be released so we can join with the One Love that we are. This liberating process leads us to project, perceive and experience a happy dream within this holographic reality. From the divine (true) reality standpoint, we are either asleep or awake; therefore, the cure is to regain Consciousness and reclaim our infinite identity.

RELIGIONS, METAPHISICS AND SPIRITUALITY INTERTWINING WITH SCIENCE

Through recent time breakthroughs and physicists' insights, we are observing an interesting merge between science and ancient wisdom. The concept of an illusory nature of reality is conveyed in many philosophies and religions in the world – from Plato's cave describing the world as shadows projected on the walls to the remarkable expansion of the concept in Hinduism and Buddhism.

The deeper we go into the great philosophers' precepts and prominent religion doctrines, the more we realize the similarities on attempting to lead us to the truth. We had substituted the philosophers for scientist; nevertheless, they are coming up with the same conclusions. Physicists are proving how all we think as solid are nothing but "empty spaces" and "holographic" and that "there is no out there, out there". Neuroscience has concluded our five senses are only signals in the brain, which are sensed in the brain a few seconds before an exterior stimulus.

Mockingly ancients should be calling us out "I told you so!"

and probably laughing at the fact we are just getting started to know the truth. The truth we have been seeking for with our brains instead of the mind and soul.

The oldest living religion, Hinduism, historically acknowledged since 1900 BCE to 1400 BCE[3] followed by Buddhism, Jainism, Taoism, and Sikhism (to name the most predominant) all regard to God as the only reality (or the Oneness) while, the so called reality, as a void, emptiness or mirage. Sounds familiar? If we translate this to a scientific terminology is like saying 'the Field' and the holographic nature of reality, respectively. Note we will distinguish the mundane from the divine-nature terminologies (like consciousness and self) by using small or capital letters, respectively.

The most prevalent ancient-religious denomination for this 'fantasy world' (collapsed Quanta or holographic reality) is Maya. Even tough this term is fundamentally rooted in Hinduism and Buddhism; Jesus often declared there was a higher realm of existence beyond this physicality, and that his reign was not of this world. The concept of Maya describes the material world as an appearance and that behind this mirage is emptiness. Hence, reality does not actually exist and, all there is out there is pure Consciousness.

Every-thing is only in the mind. Therefore, when scientists conclude 'the world out there' only exists when observed, they hit the wall at the effort to explain what actually collapses Quanta (make everything real). Here is where many of them are embracing the concept of consciousness as an answer. But be aware that

---

[3] wikipedia, history of Hinduism

the capital c Consciousness spoken by the ancients refers to our infinite, divine nature. The small c consciousness relates to our illusionary physical world, or Maya, which is merely the projector that mistakenly gives our soul a limited version of Itself through a body that identifies with a gender, age, religious background, race, nationality, social status, financial status, family values, etc. When the soul gets trapped into these false identities, lust, greed, anger and other configurations of the ego, is when we fall deep into the illusion, deep into this unconscious dream of empty atoms.

What fascinated me when noticing these spiritual/scientific connections was to realize it is all a matter of translation. Depending on the country, we call an apple manzana, mela, maçã or milo. But, at the end, an apple is an apple no matter what! Thus we can reverence the 'Christ within', the 'Krishna within', the Koran's "closer than your jugular vein" definition, the Sikh's "God is all pervading and alone dwelling in the Mind" portrayal, or plainly call the universe a Quantum soup that organizes itself in the mind, through an observer. At the end, they are all pointing out we are Infinite Possibilities, an unlimited Consciousness, or the "One" Mind of God.

"We live in illusion and the appearance of things. There is a reality. We are that reality. When you understand this, you see that you are nothing, and being nothing, you are everything. That is all"
– Gautama Buddha

At this point you may ask the same question I had: so how come this universe and everything in it FEELS so real? Answers are perceived and manifested as we practice awareness. In my case, I had this question lingering on my mind until I had my answer in an interesting and entertaining way. Our Consciousness or Source, Spirit, Higher Self, Holy Spirit or Quanta responds and communicate with us in ways we are more approachable or can better understand. My 'antennas' are often very receptive to obtain answers through movies. They are like modern day parables – Jesus' favorite means to come up with metaphors in assisting us to comprehend what was so beyond our understanding. Plus, understanding that life is but thoughts in the mind constantly processing imaginary stories, nothing more appropriate than to observe it as a fairytale. Fairytales are full of symbolisms that need to be interpreted for one's full understanding. Therefore, regarding the point about Maya (what we call reality) feeling so real, the movie "The Island" had one particular scene that made this aspect more clear to me.

The scene has Scarlett Johansson fighting her friend on a boxing ring. They are sweating, giving and receiving punches on an intense boxing match. Then the camera zooms out and we realize they are both outside the ring manipulating their holographic selves. Only the characters immersed in the hologram could feel the fight dynamics as real. Don't we all, at one point, get deeply absorbed in a good movie feeling all the emotions, until we snap out of it? Don't we all feel our night dreams real, until we wake up? This is the equivalent of what Michael Talbot concluded in the Holographic Universe. The world around us feels real because we are in it! The holographic characters feel all the hologram as real because it is their holographic universe!

Interestingly, today's movies are getting more and more helpful in illustrating "futuristic" concepts and stretch our belief system outside the box we all got raised and programmed into. As a kid, I remember watching a movie and being perplexed by a hi-tech secret-service agent speaking and solving his problem using a wristwatch. Remarkably, today we don't have to stretch our imagination and anyone can purchase a wristwatch to speak on the phone or find out how to get to the moon!

Likewise, since The Matrix phenomena, many movies are reinforcing the idea that reality is a mental construct, which is reflecting the acceptance, acknowledgement and understanding of a higher perspective of reality. Others to mention are Inception, Lucy, Transcendence, Vanilla Sky, OtherLife, The Island, Flatliners, The Discovery, Source Code, Mr. Nobody, and many others that are becoming symbols and tools to expand our narrow understanding. Technological ways to communicate globally is also making previously secret and selective information easier to be shared and aware of. So near death experiences, lucid dreaming, astral projections and hallucinogenic episodes are more widely spoken and investigated nowadays, allowing concepts of reality to broaden. For example, the many descriptions of people seeing their own bodies laying dead on a traffic accident are widening the concept we are not a body and that we do not see with our eyes. It is their consciousness that can observe, experience, and describe everything after they were declared deceased.

As said in Hinduism, the soul's ultimate aim is to experience the sole Consciousness of who we truly are - the supreme reality of Self - thus called Self-realization or enlightenment. It is a recurring idea that God is within us – complete, whole and undivided – waiting to be remembered and acknowledged. From the Greeks 'know thyself' to Muhammad 'Whoever knows himself knows God', world religions and mystical groups have delve deep into the notion of the Kingdom of Heaven being within each one of us. Bringing back to Christianity, it is no secret or surprising the fact that the Bible was put together in a censored manner, thus frequently manipulated and adulterated to conveniently benefit the system, authorities, and social conventions of the time.

The recovered 'lost Gospels of Thomas', kept by the early sects of Christianity (Gnostics), show a Jesus with a very different approach to spirituality. The traditional gospels say Jesus is the only Son of God when the lost gospel of Thomas says we are all Sons of God. This mystic gospel disagreed with much of the precepts of the emerging Christian hierarchy led by Constantine. In banned gospel, God was said to be within, thus no need for priests, bishops or commanders. In one incident when Jesus was close to be stoned to death for claiming he was God, in his defense he simply recites, "It is not written in your law, 'I have said you are gods'" - Psalm 82:6. Interestingly, this is followed by "You are all sons of the most high" - Psalm 82:7, in the Bible.

Historically, much of the early Christians were like their founder, heading to secluded journeys and attempting to achieve union and oneness with God.

This Oneness experience or enlightenment is the outcome of eradicating from the ignorance of not knowing our divine nature.

On doing so, the soul gradually escapes the restrains of Maya and moves towards liberation, or salvation.

So now that we can rationally come to the conclusion we are not this flesh but empty atoms constructed by concepts and assumptions, we can start embracing and replacing our false beliefs. This enables and entitles us to recognize our true identity as God-Creator. Like all the little pieces of a shattered hologram convey the whole hologram in each part, our seemed fragmented billions of individual minds are just shattered forms of the One Mind dreaming this human experience.

It was difficult for me to grasp this concept and it was lingering on my mind for a while. Interestingly, I got my surprising "holy assistance" not in a movie this time, but still, very elucidating. I was on a road trip to watch the total eclipse (very symbolic to get some clarity, by the way) and I was reading the Holographic Universe book in the passenger seat. Perhaps reading that book refreshed the inquiry in my mind. The National Public Radio station was on and narrating an interesting study describing episodes of many hallucinogenic drug users. Then my answer arrived. A woman that had used LSD recounts a remarkable experience where she would look at an animal and sensed everything about being that animal – she could fully feel being that animal! Then the same embodiment was felt with flowers and other human beings. She could feel one with them, one with all! I was astonished to hear it and to realize the direct message and implication it had for me. Each individualized mind (each one of 'us') is under a spell of separation and egocentric concepts.

In Genesis, the Bible says that Adam felt into a deep sleep, but never mentions him waking up. We are all one contained in his dream, on a journey to wake up and ascend. Like Neo in the Matrix, we shall free our minds. What imprisons the mind is the thought system of separation from our divine nature, and the convincing belief in this dream state as reality – which is the ego's thought system. Just like a magician act loses its enchantment when we learn how the magic trick works, so the ego loses power over us when we acknowledge the whole humanity is under its spell. Our freedom, thus called Salvation in the Course, is to remember we are all One in the Mind of God. True reality is spiritual in nature.

PART 2

LIFE PARABLES AND ITS MIRACLES

So everything around us is a subconscious projection (like a night dream) communicating in symbols. We can go through life learning by default, taking our time and hundreds of incarnations to wake up and go back to our Source for good; or, we can put effort into understanding the symbols, lessons and purpose of all we are projecting to accelerate this awaking process and make the journey less distressing.

From this point on, I will share with you some episodes of my life and how I process and put all the 'theory' into practice, as the purpose of doing the Course is not to improve our knowledge about divine truth but to bring us to the experience of the Divine Love we are.

The constant awareness of looking at life as a projection and an opportunity to see the 'false as false' (forgive) is an active meditation and a disciplined workout to transform our thought system – it is our function. The functional willingness can be compared to the efforts we set when exercising. Here the word 'exercise' comes as a meaningful metaphor. Training the mind to let go of guilt, unworthiness, shame, and fear, akin to working out the body with dozens of reps and sets of an exercise, gets proportionally easier, rewarding and joyful as time and commitment goes by. It may feel like a tough Boot Camp at first, but only until we look at it differently - and rejoice with the process and its results.

Life occurrences are thoughts in form. Accordingly, all distresses are wounds that take shape from judgments (based on personal concepts, values, believes) held in the mind. They originate from our upbringing and societal programming, but ultimately, they are fruits of the ontological guilt and fear originated from the idea to be autonomous and apart from our Creator. Once the Mind/Sonship (we) believed this happened, a holographic explosion of multiple identities and possibilities was incepted as a dream full of symbols, traps and amusements under the ego's underworld – a subconscious thought system. This dreadful spell keeps us feeling guilty, fearful and punishing ourselves. Deep questioning is fundamental to bring all these deceptions to awareness. Only consciousness can overcome this subconscious mind plot. To inquire is to uncover and release the ego dynamics for healing the mind. A healed mind perceives miracles, as miracles are not a manifestation (thought forms) but an extension of the infinite loving Mind that we are. Thus, every time we overlook egoical circumstances, we are healing the mind and perceiving miracles. Miracles are a change in perception.

I confess I enjoy analyzing and interpreting my upsets, as a psychotherapist would do. Like deciphering a night dream, it is usually a meticulous and interesting process of identifying my subconscious garbage. First I look at what feelings I am getting from the experience; second, what was I previously feeling which had me manifest that situation as a validation from my ego - thus making the subconscious story real.

The dramas I face may not seem like much to you, neither yours to me, as each 'individualized virtual reality' (personalized lesson) have a big meaning *to us* based on the meaning given *by us*. This is why, for example, your mother could drive you crazy making a comment about the weather, which will make no effect on me but, for you, will mean she is trying to manipulate how your day should be planned. We give everything a meaning based on our past associations and mental conditionings. This is why the "be in the present" is so addressed by today's non-dualistic teachers. We need to put a stop on past associations and the mental spinning wheel we recreate over and over again.

Ultimately, the only process we need to do is ask the HS for help to see (perceive) the situation differently. Subsequently, we need to trust, release our plans, judgments and recognize the only problem comes from the ontological guilt, remorse, shame and fear associated with the false belief we separated from our Primogenitor like an arrogant teenager declaring autonomy. A miraculous harmony will result from practicing a reality check to know and realize this is not so. At one point, even this process will become unnecessary and redundant and all we would do is to instantly overlook the universal hologram - not believing in the screenplay we are making up, in the first place. What delays this knowing and awakening is our deep investment in personal stories and worldly semantics – the programmed pretense we are nothing but vulnerable human-doings. We get so conditioned and afraid to let go of control that we master the art of creating defenses against our greatness. The ego has ingenious ways to make us forget the Christ (Divine Self) we truly are, but there is no value in delay!

For now, I am still going through the process of recapping we are all inside a deep sleep having a psychotic break from our glorious spiritual Reality. The stories and the process I am sharing with you are not necessarily in chronological order. For this reason, some may have more details than others. This is because as we get more clarity about the mind games and ego traps, the quicker we overlook and dismiss the whole staged show of life. The more we practice to divinely align our thinking, the more we remember we are still as God created us – innocent and perfect love. Therefore, we more rapidly immerse and experience ourselves in a happy dream of peace and joy.

As life situations keep coming to my attention, I will continue to write and share my forgiveness processes (true "reality check") in a website. Please feel free to check out BootCampInMiracles.com. Share your stories, tell how you process them and what miracles you come to experience. The ACIM needs to be experienced, otherwise is just another literature or abstract theory. Consistently applying the teachings will liberate our minds from duality and bring us back to the ultimate awareness where all is One. What we share, we strengthen. Because we are infinitely One, we are all doing this for each other and for the whole. We are literally in this together!

TERRIFYING DECISION LEAP

This is the first 'reality check process' I remember doing and the most dramatic one. I had read the book The Disappearance of the Universe, started to do the ACIM and was committed to take this journey seriously. These were my first steps looking at all as a symbolic dream or subconscious illusion, thus my process was more into the ego dynamics than the miracle content.

In this account, I had just invested a big amount of personal savings for my nutritional book to be professionally edited. For many reasons this created a great amount of fear and stress in me. Was I doing the right thing? Was this really necessary, etc? There was no turning back from here on.

The very next day I paid the editor, I was ready for another daily routine of waking up at 5am to train a client in my building. But that morning a big noise woke me up about 15 minutes before the alarm. It was a loud blast followed by a splash. There is an intersection near my building where cars crash pretty frequently, so as I suddenly woke up, my first thought was that somebody had hit a fire hydrant. I got up and went on with my morning routine. As I go down to meet my client in the gym, building employees and police officers were blocking any access to the gym, pool and common areas of that floor. I had a bad feeling as I connected some dots. I asked if someone had jumped out the balcony and they responded positively. I calmly went back to my apartment. I approached my balcony door and my whole body started to tremble. I kept telling myself this was an illusory projection of my inner condition. I stepped out but away from the balcony edge

51

so I could see downstairs only partially. I slowly opened my eyes enough to see a police officer grabbing a body out of the pool. I felt petrified. The flood of emotions was intense. I started a Q&A with myself.

Q: What are you feeling?
A: I am nervous, I am scared, I am terrified!
Q: What thoughts are coming to your mind?
A: I can't stop thinking about what was going on in his mind as he was falling! Did he regret it, as there was no turning back?

As I said this I realized how I materialized all the emotions I was previously overlooking and fighting against. There was no turning back from the decision I had made, the money I had invested and the responsibilities I had to commit to. I was afraid and terrified of the 'leap' I made and that scene was materializing all the feelings I did not want to confront. As the projection got clearer, I calmed myself down affirming and understanding this was a moment of truth and all was in divine order. I kept repeating and explaining over and over the ego mechanics of denial, projection and outside validation. I kept voicing the messages of the ACIM and trusted all things work together for good. As the truth started to sink into my mind, I got calm and astonished to witness and realize how quick-witted the ego can be towards scheming and terrifying us! The miracle is the change in perception, realizing nothing really happened that day – it was a holographic motion picture of the turmoil going on in my mind. That striking scene was a remarkable opportunity to face unhealed aspects of my mind and look at it differently. This is the purpose of the world and all our circumstances.

BIRTHDAY ASTROLOGICAL INFERNO

I have been working out for decades and this was my first careless accident in the gym. I was re-racking a pair of 50lbs dumbbells and one of them felt from the edge of the rack to the top of my left foot. It was so intense that for a few seconds I felt no pain. I immediately started to hear advice from people in the gym and someone helping me out was saying to expect at least six months to recover from it. My first reaction was to refuse all the negativity and scary prognostics. I kept praying in my mind asking for help to see that differently and to not make that real. All is well. Limping I went to a Whole Foods store and bough supplements to keep pain and inflammation at bay. I was aware I was using 'magic' but everything was so intense that I needed all the help I could get. As I kept praying for clarity "Please let me see and understand this the way You would have me do it", thoughts and images started to come into my mind. Our function in this world is to recognize the false is false (forgive) and agree to correct our misperceptions, thus disempowering the ego ambush over us. Like a puzzle, different thoughts and images crossed my mind like pieces coming together to show me what the challenge was all about.

My birthday was approaching and I was feeling nothing but discontent about it. At that time I was comparing myself to how I was years back (vigorous, fit, athletic, youthful) and evaluating how time flies. Inquiring how was I feeling with the injury, I started to get clarity within my answers. I was previously feeling extremely melancholic, frustrated and upset. I could not do anything to avoid the inevitable - getting older! I remembered thinking to myself, time goes so fast and in a few years I will be fifty years old! No wonder a 50lbs weight dropped on my foot, a symbol of my distress about walking through the unavoidable process of aging - at least while believing in linear time. But miracles can also collapse time as it weakens the power of the ego thought system. I actually witness this on my recovery after releasing this experience to the HS. All that is necessary is for us to invite and allow the Source to work through us.

There are no accidents, no coincidences, and no chances. The injury was my melancholy, frustration and upset in physical form – an external justification. I understood how I was repressing and ignoring my feelings concerning aging and how they took form as a tangible hurt that made my sorrows concrete – the outside factor to blame. Bringing my hidden fears and limiting believes to awareness started my healing process – mentally, physically, and spiritually.

Mentally, I understood the ego dynamics. Spiritually, I prayed constantly and remind myself the soul I am is timeless, ageless and I would see and use any transformations for my highest good, as I am still as God created me – perfect in any way. This body is only an image; it has nothing to do with what I am. I would constantly counteract any negative thought or concept about what I was going through with an antidote – an opposite affirmation and reflections about divine truth.

Following this consistent mindful 'workout', miracles started to unfold. As I worked on my inner state of mind, the outside world started to provide all I needed to improve my physical condition. Initially, I was using my Course affirmations and natural supplements as a magic tool; then, a client's husband that saw me limping around invited me to join him on his spinal column therapy session. Knowing my preferences and what I am comfortable with, the HS put me on the hands of a professional very attuned with non-orthodox medicine and treatment modalities like acupuncture, chiropractic biophysics and natural dietary support. After a few visits I came to know I was in hands of a brilliant young professor who has traveled the world teaching and was one of the only three professionals to own an electrical-current acupuncture machine in the country, at the time. To top it of, these innovative and expensive therapy sessions (beyond my budget) got paid by my client's husband who ended his therapy shortly after mine was over. Summing these amazing sequences of miracles, my full recovery came about a record time of one third of the anticipated time!

We cannot heal what we hide from ourselves. Pain, physical or emotional, is a selective memory communicating and reveling an aspect of the illusions we hold and thus need to forgive (recognize it is false). Watching our responses, triggers and symbols to what seems to be happening to us is essential for healing. I had a deep desire to understand the underlying aspects of my injury and pain, which allowed the HS to help me into my function, a present memory, a fresh memory. A holy instant is a memory of God, and this is our calling. The breakthrough is the use of memory unattached to the past and to remember what we truly are. This miracle working of coming to our real senses is the coming to a new form of selective memory. My process was to focus my mind in recalling my divine nature and staying present – not in the nostalgia of the past or the concerns for the future. This included reminding myself I am an immortal spirit and the body only an image of a linear construct.

Our minds hold only love, peace and joy when we stay right-minded, when we think with God. As we take responsibility for the projections of our attack thoughts, we are able to address the healing necessary in the mind. The healing of the body is subsequent. Experiencing the miracle is letting go of the disorienting web of conflicting thoughts at play.

FLOURISHING REVELATION

Appears I have been making so much effort to heal and stay right-minded that this revelation came up out of the blue. As we recognize our capacity to choose against the ego, our will, responsibility and power to forgive also increase. This next passage was eye (mind) opening for me to understand how we become a product of associations from the past.

For many years, especially as a teenager, I was a flower "Grinch" equivalent. My mom has always been a flower lover and would often buy them from the street markets. I used to criticize her saying that spending money in flowers was a waste of money as they die so quickly. I also had occasions where I told boyfriends not to bother with flowers but with something more useful instead. Yes, I know, it sounds pretty unromantic from my part. Frankly, it never crossed my mind to find out about my "attack thoughts" regarding flowers because I never saw it as anything other than a simple preference. We easily see our blocks to peace, love and beauty as nothing to it. My dislike for flowers got less intense over the years, but honestly, admiring them was never something truly authentic for me.

Recently, I was listening to Eckhart Tolle and, to make a point, he spoke about the action of picking up a flower. I am not aware of any negative thoughts while I was listening to it, but I'm sure they subconsciously crossed my mind since, suddenly, I started to get long forgotten childhood memories.

I was on a short road trip to a grape festival with my mom, dad, aunt and cousin. At one point, we stopped at a restaurant, which had an amazing forest-like land full of flowers and blossoming trees. There was a sign welcoming visitors to walk around and a notice asking people not to pick the flowers but to just admire them. As a flower enthusiast, my mother was delighted. As we walked around this flower heaven, she started to pick some of them up from the floor. As my mom kept walking and picking up flowers, my normally loud and opinionated father started to sound more and more like an annoying barking dog. I remember thinking my mom had a point; since she was not ruining the plants by picking only the ones that had already fallen on the floor. But Mr. Right kept repeating about the sign that said no picking flowers period! The ego worships being right and focus on the errors of others. This makes one feel superior and more virtuous. When we point out a 'sin' on someone else, we project our guilt to have a false feeling of relief and innocence. My dad was so loud and annoying that at one point my mother just dropped all the flowers and we left that place on a terrible note. Clueless was I to ever guess how this bitter experience would linger in my subconscious mind ever since!

I was very surprise to observe how this subliminal distress unintentionally came up to my awareness. The course says we are never upset for the reasons we think. Indeed we are always associating and reviving the past if we do not bring things up for healing!

Finally I understood my unreasonable dislike and resistance for flowers. Instead of graceful beauty, they were a visual reminder of my father's harsh personality and a symbol of misunderstandings, distress and arguments. I feel sorry it took me so many decades to clear this out from my mind, but it was an amazing way to acknowledge how we push harmony and beauty away due to early mind programming and associations. It was as if my subconscious defense mechanisms were decreeing that by disliking flowers, I would be avoiding uncomfortable and hostile experiences. Ultimately the ego is always setting us up to be deprived of beauty, love, grace, and harmony from our lives. But the source of healing to remove the shadows from love's presence is always right in our minds, where God placed it. As my willingness to admit I see things incorrectly increases, I comprehend I have a choice to either hold onto my egoical perception or recognize that only love is real by forgiving it all. With the HS help we see more and more the price we pay if we let the ego take over our life. This facilitates the atonement (mindful correction) and our decision for Heaven, which is the miraculous perception where happiness dwells.

YANNY OR LAUREL TO MY RESCUE

"Yanny or Laurel" is a computer-generated recording that went viral on social media on March 13, 2018. Incredibly, a Twitter poll had some people hearing the word Yanny and others hearing Laurel, on a near 50-50 ratio result. It was inevitably shocking and unbelievable to witness someone next to you hearing something completely different than you and, no wonder; it became an immense cyber craze.

But with all my dedication to understand how we all live in a personal virtual reality processed in the mind, it became essential for me to comprehend what was this brainteaser all about. I remember finding explanations from psychology experts that the auditory illusion (I loved the word used) happens when the brain cannot decide on exactly what it is hearing, making the sound become a "perceptual boundary". Some neuroscientists made a parallel to the Necker Cube (popularly called the face/vase illusion) describing the sound a "perceptually ambiguous stimulus". They also mention that the audio frequencies and even the shape of our ears possibly play a part on the different results. Nevertheless, the more neuroscience I would read, the more mystify I would get. This is mind-blowing and scary. It goes to show (or prove) how two people never perceive the world the same way, as the Course emphasizes!

The repercussion of this auditory illusion has been immense

to my understanding of the subjectivity of "reality" or, in other words, the universal illusion we find ourselves in. In fact, it came as a blissful response to clarify some predicaments I had in mind at the time. I was pretty upset with the ongoing political circus and all the news distortions, grotesque comments and extremely divided public views. The advantageous side of these discrepancies was that I could clearly see the delusion inside the illusion. As the scenarios were taking my peace away, I kept asking the HS to help me see things differently or through His 'eyes' (true vision). Suddenly, the Yanny/Laurel flashed my mind. How can we all ever come to full agreements on anything? In a glance, I understood how today, and throughout history, human beings have always been divided and in conflict. Hence, the Course constantly discloses how the ego thought system thrives in duality. In accordance, the Course bursts our bubble regarding accomplishing peace on Earth. Instead, it assists us to seek to change our minds about the world. We are unique individuals projecting a universe based and programmed by our own set of ego traumas and beliefs. The antidote comes by asking for true vision, which expresses miracles. Miracles, as heaven on Earth, are a change in perception.

Since then, the Yanni/Laurel phenomena has helped me, many times, to prevent my mind from continuously spin with judgments, upsets and ego dynamics against anything or anyone. It helps me to remember everything is only a sensory illusion in my mind. Thus, it is absurd to expect all or any characters in this universal hologram to perceive the world as I do.

The world is domain of the ego and as long as we keep investing in anything other than our unified divine nature, we will keep trapped in time, space, birth, death, peace, wars, right, wrong, victim, victimizer, pro-govern, anti-govern, environmentalists, polluters, happy, sad, liberals, conservatives, rebels, conformists, good and bad. We are all One in the mind of God. This is the only fact; this is the only reality. This recognition will emerge whenever we drop our rebellious existence as a separate and autonomous "self" based on fictitious concepts, desires, thoughts and beliefs that keep us blocked from reality.

While we still cling to our ego identity and the satisfaction to be right, we resist our divine Self and the opportunity to experience all without the shadows. What is required is for us to bring to light (release to the HS) our grievances, worries, expectation, demands, anger, frustrations, opinions and beliefs, which constitute our self-concept and self-image. In other words, we give up needing to be right about who we think we are and what we think we know.

A non-dualistic mindset is the escape from this paradoxical maze; it is the conscious recognition of who we truly are, and what truly exists. It is recalling that only Love is real. This is what keep us in peace and bring us the miracles.

BIZARRE DATE

It is interesting to look back and realize how our mind puts information together and responds to our vibrations, mindsets and beliefs. It is the case in this story, plus it showed me, again, not to take anything in this holographic world too seriously.

This was a time I was telling myself I needed to have a little more fun. I recognized I have not been on a date in a while, or movies, etc. I admit from time to time I miss having company at home, dressing up, having a nice restaurant meal or just checking out the hot spots in town. I asked a friend what dating app she would recommend me. I listened to a few opinions and considered joining one of them sometime soon. The next day, there was a sudden change in my schedule and I felt like driving to get some coffee at a place I usually go to. As I am getting my beverage, a friendly guy starts talking to me and we had a nice, short and fun conversation. He got my phone number and the following Friday we went out for my long sought dinner date!

To add to the magic flow of events, one day before the date, a client tells me about a new nice restaurant in town. Because of the bad weather, the suggestion was just perfect. I was grateful for the opportunity to break my routine and for all the unfolding, even though I was getting more and more clear this was about my desire to go out rather than a future relationship. Being lucid of this made me not have expectations and enjoy the evening without stress of any kind. While he was driving and talking about his day, I got many clues about his persona. A divorced middle aged man that moved from the Middle East to Miami less than five years ago, works hard, makes many investments, earns a lot of money, drives a luxury car, criticizes easily and have a strong opinion about anything and everybody. I was in such joy that not judging him was easy. All I could think was "so what"? I was not bounding, feeling chemistry or identifying with anything of true value, but I was valuing that moment.

With my cheerfulness, a car pulls out as we arrive, and we parked right in front of the restaurant, like if it was an urban fairytale. It was a rainy evening so, to avoid walking to the payment machine, I offered to pay for the street parking from my phone app. Without reservations, we walked in and immediately get seated, near the entrance. As we sat at the table, things became peculiar and oddly comic. I was trying to get the parking code when he says not to worry as the weather was bad and, sitting practically next to the car, we could keep an eye on it. The place was all glass walls so I agreed and told him to make sure to look at it every so often, as I was doing the same.

While waiting for the menu, I noticed him restless, looking around until he mentions we should get another table asserting "I" was not comfortable there. I felt he did not want to sit near the entrance, so I just ignored the ego "displacement". Looking around and observing there were no small tables available, I said there was nothing wrong with our table. As a new, trendy restaurant, people were starting to come in, so I felt there was no reason to be picky or unconsidered with their demand. With a big smile I told him I was fine and went on to point out all the positive events so far, how nice the place was, the courteous employees and so on. He acknowledged and agreed with what I said then continued saying we should ask for another table because the air conditioning was blowing on my back (I was wearing a bare back blouse) and "I" was getting cold. With a confused look and a big smile, I told him I was satisfied with the temperature and feeling no wind on my back. I went ahead to focus our attention on the menu and the food.

After a while, the maître d' approached our table and asked if the car by the door was his, and informed they were giving it a ticket. As he gets up to rush to the car I gave him my phone, telling to show the man we were trying to get the code to process the payment. After a good while, he comes back to our table and explains the man could not cancel the ticket once it was processed electronically. The man gave him a card with an email address where he could describe what happened to dispute the parking citation. I said I was sorry for that and shared I take my chances some times, no big deal. But then things became awkward and inconsistent. He started to accuse the maitre d' of purposely warning him too late, and for paying more attention to me and 'all' the women in the establishment than doing his job. I was in shock. First, I had noticed the tall and handsome guy a few times and, in no occasion, he was gazing at me. I would surely be the first one to notice if this was the case. Actuality, in all instances, I noticed him busy and very diligent with all tables and employees. Second, the restaurant became hectic and we were fortunate to have him get out of his way to respond for that matter. For a few minutes I kept pointing out the positive side of all, our nice evening and encouraging him to let it go. We were finally engaging a calm, trivial conversation when, out of sudden, he stands up and starts speaking out loud accusing the maitre d' again with all the stuff he mentioned before. I had a combination of feelings between shock, disbelief and comedy. The benefit of witnessing such an absurd scene was that I could clearly see the delusion inside the illusion. Easily forgiving the pathetic behavior, I looked at him with a big smile and said to let it go; by the way, the fish is so good, dear! I was still having a great time and enjoying the glorious evening!

It is easier to observe in a detached manner when situations are bizarre and impersonal. In this case, I was not emotionally invested in the person or the outcome. I was actually just excited to see how the universe had arranged the pompous date I had been craving for. I did not try to defend anyone, expose the absurd of his accusations, or persuade him to see the bright side of the gesture. After realizing it was pointless to do so, I kept observing how everything there was just a show for my entertainment and understanding about ego dynamics and perception.

To comprehend this lesson even more deeply, a few days later, correlated information came to my awareness. Investigating into neuroscience to understand the Yanny/ Laurel phenomena, I recalled and did some search on "the dress" craze that hit the Internet in 2015. This came as another blessing responding to my willingness to see things from a higher perspective. The polarizing viral picture of a two-colored striped dress astonished the world. The viewers were split in two groups: one seeing the dress as blue and black, and the other seeing the dress as gold and white. Particularly now, this stunned me big time. What a repercussion into the realm of perception! Neuroscientists had explanations ranging from individual's mental assumption of what kind of light was illuminating the dress (natural or artificial) to age, sex, and the amount of daylight a person is exposed to in life. This is vital information! This is an undeniable piece of evidence to conclude how our mental programming (established by environment, convictions, assumptions, and beliefs) interfere and define the world we experience. What we all witnessed with the dress wonder is the underlying fact that we cannot trust what we see, as it is nothing but our left side of the brain version of the world. This is the central ego scheme to maintain our sense of self and the separation game. Each of our minds is filling up the gaps with information that is familiar and safe to assume as true because we value our separated self. Each one of us only exists in our imagination, like a video game avatar. We cherish our persona, our life, and our world because we believe this is all real. But seeing does not make anything true, no matter how many billions of people say otherwise. Truth is beyond the self-made concepts.

If I had bitten the ego bate, my evening would have been ruined. This is why Jesus taught us not to judge. Telling my date the maitre d' was not looking at me (neither at "all" the women in the restaurant), that he was attentive to his duties and notified us with good intentions was not going to get me anywhere but into more arguments. It would be like trying to come to an agreement about "the dress" color. It is not his or my 'fault' if I see the dress as gold and white because I spent most of my life outdoors! His perception of that man was based on his cultural and personal upbringing, narcissistic needs for power and control, and the collective guilt we all share. Judgments keep the madness real and this is how the ego maintains its domain over our minds. We escape by recognizing the egoical deception. I reprimanded him for nothing, as forgiveness –the central theme of the Course - is to overlook illusions.

In the Course, Jesus is helping us to see how the mind is the cause for everything we experience. He is also showing how we can heal our ego mindset by taking responsibility for our false interpretation and releasing them for His. Awareness and willingness to perceive things with the HS starves the ego, allows true perception and provides happiness. Only our Divine Source sees above and beyond this worldly maze. Only through His guidance we are able to get out, rise above the illusion and wake up from this dream - one projection at a time.

MOM'S PHONE CALL

I usually speak to my mother on Sunday afternoons. One weekday, however, she called me late in the evening. Very surprised and sort of preoccupied, I grabbed the phone. She apologized for calling me at night as I typically go to bed early. Immediately, I could sense some stress in her voice. She started by telling me her sister had called with an inventory of criticism and insults at her. To give you a context between the two, they incredibly have complementary ego dynamics. My aunt's personality type can become hostile and controlling, while my mom's stay more silent and submissive.

My mother is about to turn eighty years old and, a while back, I encouraged her to join Facebook to keep her busy, up to date and somehow involved in the world. Hence, the reproaches directed to my mom ranged from how she "had nothing better to do in life" than to be on social media to how foolish she and her comments at posts were. To give you a context of the preliminary madness, the reason my aunt knows these facts is because her daughter is constantly on social media when she, herself, could be "doing better things with her life". My aunt's statements and arguments went on and on, and they were so grouchy, incoherent and unfair to my mother that my first reaction was to say how pathetic her discourse was. But, as we start to make corrections (atonement) a habit, the forgiveness process kicks in quickly. I bear in mind how what emerges as an attack is truly a call for love. Words started to come through me and, in absolute inspiration, I spoke for about twenty minutes making analogies and religious references in a way that my mom could comprehend. My mom does not practice the Course but, raised as catholic, she is much into Jesus and saints. Therefore, instead of looking at the symbolisms and projections that reflect back our unhealed perception, I focused on recognizing the innocence in all of us.

I started by agreeing how mistaken and unreasonable those allegations were, but instead of addressing how one was 'wrong' and the other was 'right', I continued by pointing out the innocence of both. Not doing so is what keeps us apart. Our relationship dilemmas are always opportunities to apply our function, which is forgiveness. Moments like this are when the insanity of the ego can be surrendered to the perfect Oneness – the peace and love of God.

To show her 'sinlessness', I highlighted to my mother that, as a retired professional, she has all the right to do anything she wants with her free time. Second, I addressed how her sister was unconsciously dealing with her own battles, 'life wastefulness' and unhappiness in a way she feels safe and familiar – blaming and projecting at my mother, who typically does not react in a hostile way.

The ego is ingenious with ways to deceive and make us feel righteous and superior, thus keeping us from looking inside for healing. Considering how loud and aggressive her sister gets into a discussion (typical of a frightened ego), I mentioned how dogs get very loud and annoying when they are scared. I went on to explain that when we are not disposed to look and work within, one feels unhappy, insecure, vulnerable and disturbed. The only way to manage these feelings becomes to attack and project the internal demons unto others. I added how she copes with this lack of inner work with actions that makes her look good in the world. Dealing with the façade is a quick fix to pretend and pose as someone that is good, superior, strong, and in control. These are the favorite qualities of the ego as it may come across as "positive" by society. I also suggested my mother to ask herself 'what would Jesus do' in any difficult situations. He would surely see my aunt's innocence and have compassion for her belief in being unable to turn her demanding life situations around. She is unaware to notice she is receiving all the hurt she is sending out. We all do this, one way or the other, so recognizing the need for more kindness, understanding, compassion and forgiveness would bring peace, happiness and healing for all involved. Our goal is to see light in our brothers, so we can experience it in ourselves. Forgiveness reveals new perception. To offer these blessings is to receive the same blessings. I finalized by saying we should pray for her. It was a magical experience of being inspired (in-spirit) and letting those words be spoken through me. In the process, I was definitely also paying attention to the message directed to myself.

The following day, I get another call from my mother. I was in disbelief and amazement with what she had to say: a miracle had occurred! Despite my aunt's notorious prideful personality, she benevolently called my mom to apologize and tell her how much she loves her. What a beautiful holy instant where two people joined for the purpose of healing a wound. When we ask for help and decide to join with the HS to heal a relationship, we are fully supported by the power of divine Love, which, ultimately, is what we really are.

DIET TRANSITION NIGHTMARE

This was perhaps one of the most distressing forgiveness lessons I recall and one I am still working on it. To put things into context, I was raised in a healthy eating environment. Following my divorce; I also became a conscious consumer avoiding animal foods and products. Looking back I have to admit these standpoints inflict more judgments, rules, discrimination and separation that one can bargain for. I only became aware of this by listening to the uncompromising teachings of David Hoffmeister, not only because they were true, but also because he had been in this side of the spectrum. It was easier for me to accept and respect his categorical wisdom knowing about his life. He personally was a sportsperson, vegetarian, environmental activist, nuclear protester, peace advocate and social equality supporter. My identification with David's past values not only diminished my resistance toward his radical teachings, but also made me rethink my positions, realize the ego traps of 'good concepts' and believe dropping them were attainable. Therefore, I started with my efforts and progressively begin to relinquish from diet concepts and exercise routines. This may not sound like much for many of you, but keep in mind these were deep rooted beliefs that shaped my personality and gave me a great deal of sense of self - personally and professionally.

Little by little, I started to loosen from these aspects of my identity. I remember buying cheese after years of not doing so. I watched all my thoughts and images of factory farms and animal exploitation. They were so intense that I started by getting the European milk products figuring the animals there have better lives than the ones in American milk industry. My viewpoints were so ingrained that I had to slowly loosen from them. Soon after, I started to eat eggs and fish.

Old thought patterns are like a lifelong addiction. Depending how slow or abruptly we decide to quit; we may experience a proportional setback. Like a drug withdrawal or hangover, we may get a set of life circumstances that may feel like a nightmare. And this is how my next parable goes.

I have clients at different parts of town and was on my way near the legendary Biltmore Hotel in Miami. This residential area is pretty peaceful and surrounded by old trees, waterways, golf courses, and small animals. One morning, I am driving not far from my destination when I see a horrifying scene on the street. I see a duck that got hit by a car surrounded by frantic young ducks and one adult hysterically flapping its wings and quacking in grief. As an animal lover, I can't describe my pain. It felt like a knife going through my heart. I started to pray out loud repeating over and over for help to see this differently. As thoughts of anger and sadness surfaced, I kept praying to understand this horrible projection of my mind. Before entering my client's house I did my best to recompose and minimize the painful emotion that had taken over me. On my way back through the same street, I avoided looking at the scene and kept praying, almost in tears, for help to see and understand that experience differently. About an hour later, I am driving across downtown for my next appointment. I stopped at a red light and, as I look to my right side, I noticed one cute Eurasian dove desperately jumping and flapping its wings. The dove seemed in so much agony. As I worried how distressed the dove was, I noticed another dove dead, apparently also hit by a car. I was in shock and disbelief how this was happening again! This time I was unable to hold my composure. I started to cry and scream in the car asking why was I seeing and going through this horrible pain again? What was going on inside me to perceive this nightmare outside me? What kind of attack, pain or guilt was I projecting? What was all the grief and suffering all about? Later that day, I started to get insights about the reasons for those parallel projections. I understood that, for a while, I was transitioning away from vegetarianism by eating eggs, dairies and some fish. I recalled that a few days before these incidents, I had eaten chicken for the first time after many years. By not putting too much attention to how disturbing this was to my subconscious identity, I then submerged myself in those incidents where I could blame other people for being negligent, unconcerned, murderers and causing suffering on animals. Images are a distracting device not to look inside and become merely puppets of the ego mind. Our world is a projection screen made as a defense against hidden guilt. As these mechanisms became more apparent, I started to clear this data of cause and effect in the world. I started to forgive my self and the world that seemingly formed around me. To forgive is to stop making all real and shed light to the fact that the world is not doing things to me – the world is being done by me. By asking for help, guidance and forgiveness, we are getting assistance from our divine source (outside the ego thought system that created the pain) to perceive all for what it is, a structured illusory trap made by memories.

It took me days to write about this occurrence. I am very aware is not easy not to make all this real, thus I still need healing and more clarity how to proceed with my eating habits. But thinking is of the ego domain, and the ego knows all our weaknesses to get us sucked into the illusion. As I kept deliberately forgiving and reflecting about my lesson, I had another miraculous message that gave me the clarity, reassurance, mind freedom and empowerment I needed to face this ingenious ego ambush. I am still very grateful and astonished how this helpful figurative communication came about. Saturday afternoon I decided to go to the pool for a little bit. I usually have a few books in my beach bag that I read from time to time on relaxing occasions. I grabbed The Holographic Universe and resumed reading from the page the clip was indicating I had stopped last. To my amazement, the physicist author was remarking a conversation with his professor where they were exploring a narrative from Castaneda's book. Walking across a desert with his shaman friend, they encounter a strange creature curling in a seemingly agonizing death. Observing the creature, it had the body of a calf, the ears of a wolf and a face with a beak; he immediately reacted by saying "this cannot be". As he approached the animal, he then saw it was just a big tree branch. In relief, he pointed out the confusion he had made. The shaman responded by telling him there was a spirit creature dying there but his disbelief about the creature's authenticity transformed it in something else, something he would identify as real. He then pointed out that both appearances coexist in parallel realities. Wow. This was so profound and meaningful for my ongoing personal healing regarding this sensitive subject. We collapse the quantum field into reality based on our pre-conditioned mind.

The good news is that, no matter what sin we think we committed, what guilt we endured, or what problems we have created; there is no order of difficulties in miracles. With a clear understanding of how the ego schemes everything up, we can take responsibility for our interpretations and choose to only accept what is truly real, to accept only what comes from the presence of love. The world "out there" is neutral until we give it a meaning. What we see is either our ego thoughts projected and reflected back to us, or a non-judgmental extension of innocence and perfect love. Correspondingly, I have to acknowledge and be willing to give up everything that sustains my story for murderous thoughts, grief, sadness, melancholy and despair. The ego's strategy is to keep us confined in sin and guilt and make all we see real. But all circumstances we orchestrate in life can be used to undo the ego's script and be released to the HS for our liberation, what the Course calls salvation. This holy instant of lucidity (atonement and forgiveness) is what brings us healing and true happiness. Healing and salvation of the mind comes from stopping the ego's momentum to face our feelings and beliefs. A miracle is allowing the mind to get transformed and perceive things differently.

I still value analyzing the problems, the lessons and what I probably did 'wrong'. But Jesus says we do not have to waste so much time doing so. Our efforts should simply focus on the purpose to forgive the falsehood of everything, no matter the shape or form of our trials. This simplicity took me back and reminds me of the teachings of Ho'oponopono, where we take full responsibility for what we see and judge outside of us. All the focus goes on cleaning the memories of fearful thoughts and judgments to be replaced and transmuted by love in action.

The subjects of diet and cruelty are still very substantial and delicate to me. I am still working on it and what is coming to me recently is to pay attention about what I 'feel' like eating, and then work on clearing all the terrifying thoughts and associations it may occur. If I desire something I judged as 'wrong' in the past, I will ask myself what are the reasons to eat or to not eat this? I use any feelings and thoughts that come up as a sensor to identify the beliefs I need to unwind from, the false concepts I need to forgive, and the truth I need to remember.

"Everything in this cosmos is part of
a distractive device to keep you from
remembering who you are. And whatever
made this mesmerism, this hallucination, is
pretty clever. This cleverness goes way beyond
personal. This is the kind of cleverness that
made up a whole world of unreality and

convinced the mind that it is something else
than what it is. It convinced the mind that it is
limited instead of infinite and it is flesh instead
of Spirit. Once you get a glimpse of that, then
comes the listen-and-follow part because the
same presence that created you as Spirit will
guide you to unwind your mind from this
'clever' idea. It will take you back to the Source."
David Hoffmeister

ONE PLEA, MANY REVELATIONS

This account was a good message on how not to take anything
personal and how everything is a personal lesson. This was indeed
an excellent one, full of deep information, insights and healing.

One Sunday, a guy from my Course group got very outspoken
and angry about some incidents in his neighborhood and in
society. I completely understood his reaction, as I occasionally
respond with irritation to political news that catches me by
surprise. The stronger we identify with the ego-based concepts
we are defending, the more difficult it can be to release and heal.

The issue the man was bringing up was regarding someone
he saw being gunned down and killed while policemen are not
questioned or held responsible for anything. I completely agreed
and pointed out I have done a lot of inner work regarding police,
watching and correcting my immediate thoughts when observing

them. It is not easy but we have to always remember our function to recognize it as a trap and forgive.

Unexpectedly, he reproached my reflections and one phrase hit me on the face: "There is no way I can look at that body and those policemen and say it is not real". I understand we can't just brush it off with quotes, but I was hopeful we would go through a process of expressing and healing what was underneath that rage. I truly felt sad for the denial statement because the spirit cannot act on us without our permission and willingness. Light can't enter inside a sealed container. It was the end of the meeting so I remember pointing out that, in situations we find hard to see beyond the illusion, we need to pray and ask for help to perceive it differently. We can't do it alone, especially in difficult cases where personal identity and past associations are so intricate in our psyche. Unfortunately, I sensed the message was received in disdain.

I truly felt I wanted to help, without metaphysically ghosting (solely preaching or quoting the Course), but by contributing with something that could modify his perspective, like the famous image of the vase and the profile of two faces. Once we are shown both sketches are there, it turns out easy to see one or the other.

How can I re-interpret the eyes do not see, but the brain is told what to see? Or we only see the past, the familiar? Since that Sunday, the desire to help stayed with me and a desire that keeps recurring is a prayer that we plead. This is so certain that, throughout the week, I felt all the channels and messages coming my way. First, I opened The Holographic Universe later that day. Because it is not an easy read, I only pick this book up occasionally. I should not be surprised by now but, to my amazement, I read a passage that was clearly an answer to my prayer! The physicist author narrates an account where a hypnotist was hired to entertain a group at a house party. A friend of his father became the subject and I will share with you what is relevant to this topic. After the astonishing hypnotic session, the hypnotist master tells the man he will be woken up, but his daughter will appear invisible to him, until commanded otherwise again. The man is sitting on a chair and another chair is placed in front of him where his daughter then sits. The man open his eyes, communicates and interacts with everybody in the room except to the daughter sitting right in front of him. The master is standing behind her and the chair. With all the party attendants around, the master takes a clock from his pocket and places it behind the daughter's back. He asks the father (who is looking straight at him without acknowledging her presence) to tell him what time is it and what name he sees in the clock. To everybody's disbelief and amazement, the father leans towards the man's hand and gives the precise information! Imagine me reading this, baffle and perplex not only about the incredible account, but also for the miraculous response, contribution and validation given to myself to pass it on. The following Sunday, I blissfully shared this narrative and added some insights. I pointed out how we are all experiencing a type of hypnosis. Aren't we all under a huge spell? And who is hypnotizing us? The ego is a great and ingenious hypnotic master dictating everything about our perception, from the subconscious. The ears do not hear, the eyes do not see, they are simply decoding a guiding system of suppressed pain, guilt and fear behind the images until we decide to choose a different master, to choose the HS!

Many were stunned and pleased with the conclusions and message we were able to grasp from it. But, for my surprise and disappointment, the man I so eager wanted to help turned around in full attack saying he wanted nothing to do with my Quantum Physics and hypnotist story. Plus, he emphasized he did not need help and asked somebody else to leave him alone. I let the aftershock pass and the message sink in. I then understood that the entire search was for myself. Indeed, to give is to receive as the Course says. I truly wanted to enhance the guy's perception and I ended up expanding my own mind, strengthening my trust and understanding more about this journey. I was so grateful for that blessing, seemingly in disguise. And this was not the end of it. Two days later, I got more information and clarity, which increased my awareness and blissful feeling. I randomly picked a Ken Wapnick audio and fast-forward towards the end and bam! It was so magical; all I was listening was pertinent and relevant to the situation. In short, he emphasized how all injustice we come across is the root of all judgments in the world. It holds the belief we are apart and different, where one is innocent and the other a sinner. Differences imply dualism, conflicting views, attack and the conclusion we are not one. All differences entail attack, including the ones we judge positive. If I see you as a 'wonderful person', the ego interpreters you are 'better than me'. The ego takes the message that I am being unfairly treated. Denial is the ego's primitive defense. If I prove you are sinful, I am proving I am sinless, and the ego has tricky ways to bring up darkness and set the stage up. In this case, it was about disrespect, abuse of authority, discrimination, and cruelty. More ingenious is to know it is always about the content, not the form. Here is where the ego can catch us big time! In a practical example, it is easy to set the stage to be right and innocent accusing someone to be a drug addict, when one can have a strong addiction to shopping, material things, status, looks, or financial gains. Finding a scapegoat justifies my attack on others and evades God's attack on me. Before we shout out for justice, we need to ask the HS for help to see how unjust, unkind or unmerciful we are. Justice corrects the interpretation where injustice arises.

We believe we are different, thus we work hard to portray we are better than the other. Many times, all plays out in a graphic or dramatic ways. The only purpose is for the spirit to bring up the unconscious darkness, as nothing can be healed if pushed down and hidden away. Without awareness there is no healing. Looking at the ego is how the ego gets undone. Those are the times to face the beliefs in powerlessness and brutality to make the mind ready for forgiveness. Forgiveness is the process to undo the false belief that there is a world outside of us. There is nothing out there but our own thoughts taking shape. I recognize this is a radical concept, but is one that becomes more and more evident as we exercise our function and heal. There are no winners or losers, sinful or innocent. Fundamentally, we can say the only winner is the one who remembers he is one with God. Sometimes we just need a wakeup call – a big purge to let it all out for healing.

RELATIONSHIP ASSIGNMENT

I will do my best to keep this brief, as you know relationship stuff can be very meticulous and complicated. If we think about it, there's no better way for the ego to feed itself as with people interacting with each other.

When I went to the Utah retreat in 2017, I was very determined to practice the Course and unwind from my self-identity, which is the purpose of its teachings. Not surprising, I met someone with the same mindset. We immediately "clicked" and to make a long story short, a few weeks later he came to Miami to stay with me. He was not into any lease contracts and had sold his RV, thus the situation was perfect to surrender to a relationship assignment. Both of us were thriving to follow the Course in an uncompromising way and were very inspired by the Living Miracles Community and retreat in Utah. We vowed to join and help each other in our purpose to unwind the mind from the voracious ego structures. Always be careful with what you ask for!

After a little over one month of this "Course application" and "intensive mind training" many things showed up as projections, masking and attacks that may usually go unnoticed on impersonal relationships. On special relationships, however, there are not many places to run to. I could go on and on with a list of things that popped up but I will tell you the main themes for each one of us. They interestingly show how no two people attract each other in vain. Both of us ended up flaring up what and how we were feeling in an inevitable and explosive expression-session.

In resume, I was feeling taken advantage of, manipulated

and psychologically abused. At his end, he was feeling unloved and totally unwanted in my house. We both had a list of things to justify and validate how we felt. This was a huge lesson for me because not only I strongly felt issues from my childhood coming up but I also understood the other side of the dynamic, which helped me feel less guilty about how turbulent all ended up. I clearly saw how his maneuvers "forced" me to act like I did, so he could be a victim, and I grasped how my subconscious ego also had its own strategies to put me in a victim position. The ego is indeed ingenious! He ended up leaving and running all the way to California. But the important thing was to, at one point, stop the judging, the grievances, and the hiding behind my defenses, which obscure myself from the love that I am - the love that we all are. As 'people' here on this planet, we are only characters on a screen (dream) playing out a role with other characters that have their own stories to play out. An episode like this is showing me I still believe in the story I was a little girl who was manipulated by two adults who could not deal with their own problems alone, seemingly causing a psychological turmoil I would carry in my mind for years. In equivalent ways to his childhood, the person staying with me also recalled his own traumas. It is not easy to be grateful for those events when they are occurring, but that is the only way to know the guilt, fear, false beliefs, and pains we are still hiding from the spotlight to heal.

These are the moments to release the blocks of the awareness of love's presence to the HS or Divine Source to be forgiven and transmuted, which is what precedes miracles. If I go on with details about my story to justify my anger and rest my case how unfairly treated I was, then no healing is possible. This blocks the love to flow through us, and the spirit to work its healing. Clinging to the ego's script prevents the gifts that forgiveness (memory cleaning) offers us. As I write this I still have things coming up. This means I still have healing to do. And here is where I am also applying the simplicity of Ho'oponopono that reminds us how personal stories are only data or memories we need to clean (correct and release) from the mind. Cleaning and forgiveness are the same; however, at this point I like the simplicity of just saying "Thank you" (for bringing this up) and "I love you" (remembrance of our Holy nature).

Investing in the ego keep us separated. When we take responsibility and release our judgments and attack thoughts to the light (Divine Source), we open space in the mind for love to flow and bring miracles into our experience. Every event and every encounter is perfectly orchestrated for our highest good. When we commit to heal the mind from memories of guilt and fear (personal and ontological), everything becomes an opportunity to do so. This brings a joyful perception and the expression of miracles in life.

GROCERY STORE FLASH FORGIVENESS

This is about a 'grab and go' visit to the grocery store that turned out to be a 'look and learn' how the ego set things up. It also strengthens the idea I said before that the more we exercise our function to forgive (undo the belief there is a world outside of us), the more becomes evident it is all a trap, and the easier the process for healing (from projection to forgiveness) unfolds.

There is a small neighborhood grocery store I sometimes stop by on my way home. In the years I was writing my book on nutrition, I used to imagine myself on a collaborative teamwork with that small grocery chain, as the basic concept of my work was to avoid food waste for the sake of more nutrients for people and less trash in the environment. It was also a win-win profitable setting for food retailers as food waste cost money. In brief, food waste was a sensitive and substantial subject for me, which benefit people, environment and economy.

A few days ago, I decided to stop at this market before heading home. As I parked the car and walk towards the entrance, a frantic guy started to shout and throw papayas on the floor. My automatic reaction was to feel anguish and walk towards him in reproach. As I walked watching the scene, a million thoughts came flooding through my mind; from the hungry people that could be eating those wonderful fruits to the amount of money it was costing the store. I caught myself being taken by those old ideas, but because of the peculiar correlation, I was able to quickly recognize the bizarre ego trap. Anything that takes our peace away is an alarm warning we have a subconscious assumption to deal with. But the more we observe our feelings and thinking, the more the ego is enable to hide in the darkness of our mind. Healing derives from our willingness and surrender to see things differently. Thoughts are the cause of our emotions. Underneath the images we see, there are core believes that are nothing but thought patterns. We are responsible for our state of mind, for how we react to the projections, which are there for a reason – to be seen, recognized and forgiven.

Because core beliefs are thought patterns that stay out of awareness, I wondered why this had resurfaced in the first place. When sitting down to write this, I comprehended the root of it. A few hours before I made my stop at the store, someone I haven't seen in over a year asked me about my nutritional book. I gave a quick reply and forgot about it going through my day. But the ego subconscious doesn't miss anything! It made sure to bring up my super-hero qualities and old values of helping people, saving the environment and improving food commerce. We sure stuff and hide a bag full of wasteful beliefs! It does not matter how nice or positive our justifications are, any investment in the illusion is a compromise. These are the critical and holy moments to choose differently and ask the HS for help to perceive the situation through our right mind. The symbols of the projection and my function are to forgive! As we release, we experience the Peace of God.

PECULIAR ARMS INJURY

As I am writing this, I am going through the healing stages of a curious injury. Last month, I got distracted in the gym and let go of a weight machine in a brisk way. I ended up straining my left hand and forearm. I joked around saying it was karma for wishing Argentina to loose the game they were playing at the World Cup at the time I got hurt. Considering there could be some truth and guilt in the joke, I applied forgiveness on myself and in all foolish concepts we put on our brothers. After a few days of limiting exercises in the gym, the sprain subsided and a tiny ball formed between my pinky and ring fingers. It was nothing major, but pretty painful to the touch. Just like how we do with minor issues in life, I did not bothered to question any meanings. But any sort of pain is information regarding mind and soul alignment.

About two weeks later, I was lying in bed reading and supporting my head sideways. Insignificant as it may sound, the following day I could hardly use my right arm to hold anything. It was painful, aggravating and, needless to say, the universe got my attention! Finally I was willing to question the meaning my ego was plotting against me. I started to pray for the HS to see things differently and to understand the reason of all of it. I kept releasing the situation but things did not become clear in one day. It took some time, attention and commitment.

Prior to these "minor" injuries that got me frustrated, preoccupied and upset, I was "slightly" frustrated, preoccupied and upset with my slow work situation. I was also "fairly" frustrated, preoccupied and upset how I was managing my daytime schedule. Are you getting my hint?

To be more specific, it was summertime and most of my clients were out of town. Even though this was hurting me financially, I saw this as a good opportunity to trust and devote to my writings. But between my personal workouts, errands and futile tasks, I was feeling my days were passing by in vain. I started to get frustrated and upset at myself for not being more productive and dedicated to my new book. I was dissociating from my purpose with pointless activities. A split mind is never in harmony, thus what else can we perceive and experience but disharmony? From this ambivalence, the injuries became a tool to facilitate and allow me to put priorities into perspective. The body is a communication device and when we keep ignoring the cues, the means to catch our attention can get more notable and painful. We do this to ourselves when we entrust to the soul's script but do not follow up. Purpose aligns and harmonizes the body, mind and spirit; however, it is crucial not to identify with the ego or the body, as they are both only illusions supporting each other. Ego is only a thought of self-sufficiency hence, cure comes when we turn away from it (and its foolish requirements), let go, delegate and follow our highest call. It is turning away from a Newtonian cause-and-effect view of the world to a Quantum vision of effect preceding cause. In practical example, quantum healing is to recognize my injury was not the reason for my evident pain and frustration; but my suppressed mental pains and frustrations got trans-formed into an injury. This is how the body becomes a learning device, some physical evidence that points to where correction is needed. This corrections is what the course calls Atonement. The source of pain is always in the mind. This is why Jesus reminds us that health is inner peace.

An approach I find interesting to take is to explore and decode what life is throwing at me like a night dream. Dreams are subconscious communications that expose suppressed feelings. Likewise, everything we experience in life is a dream-like collapsed quanta projected from our mind, for our awareness. When something significant happens and catches my attention (like a car problem, a duck on the sidewalk, or a fish that dies) I enjoy looking at the symbols. Sometimes I just pay extra attention and question the feelings coming up, other times, I do a deeper research. For example, I ended up having problem with both arms. What comes up when I think about arms? I think about embrace, reaching out. I understood I was upset at myself for not embracing my writings more diligently. Furthermore, my exercise routines were reducing my available time and my injuries forced me to stay away from the gym. This is helpful to understand how we must always trust the divine order of the HS script. Judging the occurrence as 'bad' would keep me on the vibration of fear, anger and guilt, thus not empowering my body and mind to forgive (recognize the subjectivity) and heal.

For more details, I sometimes check on dream interpretations. In this case, that painful little ball inside my hand (cyst like) was the most annoying. It was located right bellow my pinky finger, which represents mental power, intellect, memory, and the power of communication. The body indeed can communicate in peculiar and emblematic ways. As I became more and more aware of the injury's surreal nature, I started to feel better and even got a powerful pressure points spot massage from a colleague who is very knowledgeable in sports injuries. The help we need arises from the level we are at. It could have been an instant healing, but I am not there yet. As a matter of fact, when an ego though crossed my mind about not being faithful or spiritual enough to get healed instantly, I corrected myself and accredited this 'conventional process' as another lesson and opportunity to reach out for help and join with my 'brother'.

Ultimately, our pain, frustration, anger, guilt and fear spring from the belief we are confined to a human condition apart from our divine source (Mind of God). Holding on to an illusory world and an insignificant personal self, when we are a perfect and eternal creation, is a terrible bargain. In other words, choosing to stay asleep (in the ego virtual reality) over waking up (recognizing our divine reality) is a dreadful compromise that will always lead to suffering. Salvation (self-realization), which is the ultimate healing, is no compromising of any kind.

ADDRESSING AND HEALING UNWORTHINESS

I am on my final writing stages and was realizing I soon should be able to send away my manuscript for evaluation and editing. On the surface I appear calm and certain, but deep inside I feel some discomfort. After these thoughts and concerns, an interesting sequence of events came up as if poking my attention for healing aspects of unworthiness in my mind.

What you will see next, in italic, is an email I sent to an ex-boyfriend of more than 20 years ago. We briefly reconnected about five years ago and we haven't spoken since then. When I was having those thoughts about finishing and sending out my manuscript, I get a call from him, out of nowhere. He mentioned I crossed his mind as he was recalling memory of ours, thus he decided to call and say hi. On our quick phone conversation, I mentioned about my book and, as a writer himself, he offered to read fractions of it, if I wished. When we hanged up, I was pleased with the conversation but very aware this had a meaning. I could sense different feelings inside me; part of me was honored someone like him could help me with constructive criticism, but soon, a louder voice was terrifying me inside. I sensed a slight panic imagining such an articulate person putting up with my ordinary writing. This was a great opportunity to face my fears, my emotions of inadequacy, and put them all into new perspective.

He texted me his email address and I noticed a strong sense of obligation and 'attack' towards him, which I soon realized was my resistance and fear of the healing to come. I also comprehended how many times we become hostile towards another person, or 'too busy' or even ill to avoid facing our defense mechanisms. Refusing to look inside to heal dims our light and sends a self-message of lack of integrity that can hurt us deeply – emotionally and physically. Yes, our afflictions essentially manifest as excusing validations to put an innocent victim mask. Resistance shows up in many ways and forms. I realized all these emerging reactions were a challenge to succumb, or not, to an ego trap. As we take responsibility and welcome healing, the door opens to new awareness. Even if the opening is only a little crack, the light gets invited in!

I am sure what I am identifying is not "all there is" from this lesson, but so far this is what I have to share with you. Usually, having a mighty companion to talk to is an elucidative experience but, in this case, typing all that was coming up became a very therapeutic tool. It helped me to point, sort out and release my inner tribulations. After two hesitant days, I wrote him this email, attaching a section of my book for his evaluation:

Dear Xxxxxx!

I want to tell you again I was delighted to hear your voice again after so long. I am glad you followed your "inner guidance" to call me.

I want to share something with you. On Wednesday I was working on my manuscript and I was thinking about a word in Portuguese. I looked up the translation and the word was "eloquent". This is because I was reflecting that I read, listen and learn so much, but I wish I were more eloquent to express and share all the information more effectively. The next morning, I am with a friend and she is telling me about an interesting video she was watching, when she mentions how eloquent the guy was. For some reason this caught my attention and the word kept lingering on my mind. Later that day you call me. I have to tell you that besides distinguishing you as kind and intelligent, I find you extremely eloquent! This caught my attention again and I could not ignore there was something here. There are no coincidences!

I am learning how to pay attention to all feelings, labels and judgments we commonly ignore, as they are all ego components to keep us from healing the mind. I realized the word 'eloquent' was coming out because of my fears of inadequacy, of not being good enough, smart enough, spiritual enough, etc, to write about miracles. I recognized how hesitant I feel sending my manuscript to you because of self-condemnations. I now understand this is an opportunity to face my fears and correct these ego false perceptions in my mind. I also see the miraculous gift I am receiving of not only healing this aspect from my mind, but to also have an "eloquent person" go over my material to make it better and myself more confident about what will I send to the publisher, and the 'public'.

With this said, please understand this is a journey of unwinding the mind back to our Source/God/true Self, therefore, feel free to have no private thoughts and no "people pleasing" about what you are about to read. I will work on taking nothing personal. For me, this is a lesson, an opportunity to heal and to join with you on a beautiful purpose. Everything you have to add, suggest or criticize will be welcome for these intents.

I am sending you the first few pages, which are more personal. Later are my highlights on Quantum Physics and psychology relevant to my understanding of the Course. Then part 2 is more practical 'life tales' where I put the theories into analysis and apply them in each circumstance. I don't want to thrown all at you at once, so please keep me posted how it goes. Perhaps I can send you one of the 'tales' later on.

*Thank you again for your support and for
answering this call for love <3
Looking forward to hear from you.*

*Blessings
Monnica*

We overcome, evolve and heal by keeping nothing hidden
from awareness. By being honest and verbalizing my emotions, I
am bringing my darkness to the light. My friend kindly replied
my email to let me know he would read as soon as possible. The
next day, he called with a sincere and encouraging feedback.
His comments have been a nice symbol of support and a great
indication of a healed perspective. I also reinsured myself not to
forget I am not doing this to have a successful book; I am doing
this for myself, to teach what I still need to learn. The purpose for
this work is to keep my mind focused on awareness, alignment,
discipline, and healing. Thus I prayed and released all my mental
ambiguities to the HS. All our feelings of unworthiness originate
from the belief we broke away from our loving divine source, our
belief we separated from God.

Reviewing the sequence of events, I am grateful for: One,
this was an opportunity to be aware of how I was diminishing
myself. We cannot thrive with hidden beliefs dictating our life.
We cannot give joy and share light without stopping to make
shadows. Playing a little victim telling myself I am not smart,
spiritual or eloquent enough is a false sense of self. We can justify
a sunshield protects us, but why hide on the shadow when we
are the sun itself? Second, this was an occasion to put aside

any pride and have the humility to make amendments when necessary. Welcoming his feedback I set ground to heal arrogance, unworthiness and victimhood to give room for my light to shine. In a practical way, I was revising the material to be harmonic and, in a spiritual way, I was removing the blocks to the awareness of love's presence in my life.

Any circumstance we do not feel peaceful is a lesson, an opportunity to remind our self of the truth. As we step back and let Him lead the way, we are blessed. It takes faith and commitment, but once we receive the blessings, we inevitably extend them to everything and everyone we encounter.

"Our deepest fear is not that we are inadequate.
Our deepest fear is that we are powerful beyond measure"
Nelson Mandela

BIBLIOGRAPHY

1. https://en.wikipedia.org/wiki/Double-slit_experiment

Printed in the United States
By Bookmasters